read, think, pray, live

*G o    A h e a d :*

# TH1NK: *about God*

### *about life*

### *about others*

Faith isn't just an act; it's something you live—something huge and sometimes unimaginable. By getting into the real issues in your life, TH1NK books open opportunities to talk honestly about your faith, your relationship with God and others, as well as all the things life throws at you.

Don't let other people th1nk for you . . .

TH1NK for yourself.

# read, think, pray, live

a guide to reading the bible in a new way

by tony jones

*TH1NK Books*
*an imprint of NavPress*®

NAVPRESS
P.O. Box 35001
Colorado Springs, CO 80935

The Navigators is an international Christian organization. Our mission is to reach, disciple, and equip people to know Christ and to make Him known through successive generations. We envision multitudes of diverse people in the United States and every other nation who have a passionate love for Christ, live a lifestyle of sharing Christ's love, and multiply spiritual laborers among those without Christ.

NavPress is the publishing ministry of The Navigators. NavPress publications help believers learn biblical truth and apply what they learn to their lives and ministries. Our mission is to stimulate spiritual formation among our readers.

ISBN 1-57683-453-0

Cover design by BURNKIT

Creative Team: Jay Howver, Vicki Newby, Nat Akin, Darla Hightower, Glynese Northam

Some of the anecdotal illustrations in this book are true to life and are included with the permission of the persons involved. All other illustrations are composites of real situations, and any resemblance to people living or dead is coincidental.

Unless otherwise identified, all Scripture quotations in this publication are taken from *THE MESSAGE* (MSG). Copyright © 1993, 1994, 1995, 1996, 2000, 2001, 2002. Used by permission of NavPress Publishing Group. Other versions used include: the *New Revised Standard Version* (NRSV), copyright © 1989, by the Division of Christian Education of the National Council of the Churches of Christ in the USA, used by permission, all rights reserved.

CIP Data Applied For

Printed in Canada

1 2 3 4 5 6 7 8 9 10 / 07 06 05 04 03

FOR A FREE CATALOG OF
NAVPRESS BOOKS & BIBLE STUDIES,
CALL 1-800-366-7788 (USA)
OR 1-416-499-4615 (CANADA)

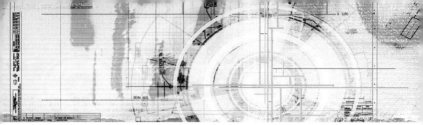

# CONTENTS

PART FOUR. EXERCISES IN LECTIO DIVINA

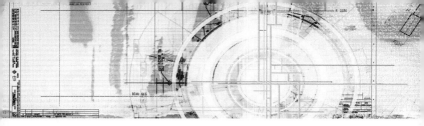

# PREFACE

Welcome into a mystery. Welcome to an ancient *and* modern way of listening for God in your life. In the coming pages, you'll run into some old Latin words. You'll read about some believers who lived long before you and me. You'll also see how this ancient method of prayer holds great promise for us, living in the noisy twenty-first century like we do.

Let's get to those Latin words right away. *Lectio divina* is Latin for "sacred reading." You probably recognize the English words *divine* and *divinity* as forms of *divina*. Sure enough, they come from the same root word. Though not quite as obvious, *lesson, legend,* and *election* come from the same root word as *lectio*.

Lectio divina has four steps, and you'll find out more about them in the coming pages. Because they began during the time when Latin was the language of the church, the steps are still known by their Latin names. They are

- *Lectio* [LEHK-tsee-o]: a selection or a reading,
- *Meditatio* [meh-dih-TA-tsee-o]: thinking over or meditation,

- *Oratio* [o-RA-tsee-o]: speaking or praying (words like *orate* and *oral* have the same root word as *oratio*), and
- *Contemplatio* [con-tem-PLA-tsee-o]: contemplation.

Don't be intimidated by these words even though they're Latin. They may make lectio divina seem mysterious — that's okay — but they're nothing more than words to describe the different stages of this type of prayer.

Now that we have that out of the way, I hope you can immerse yourself in what's ahead. Lectio divina has been a great discovery for me and for the students in my youth group over the past few years. I can honestly say that every time we've used lectio divina as a group, students have been blown away at how clearly they've heard from God during the process.

It's going to take some practice and some discipline, but I know you're up to it. Give it a try; maybe even make it a part of your daily time with God. I think that you, too, will be amazed at how God speaks to you.

TJ

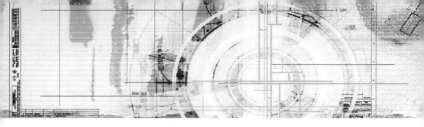

# ACKNOWLEDGMENTS

My thanks to Jay and Jen Howver at NavPress for the opportunity to write about these things that are so much a part of who I am. Thanks also to the students whom God has placed in my care at Colonial Church. And thanks to my wife Julie and to our kids, Tanner and Lily, for their support, faith, patience, and love. May God bless you all!

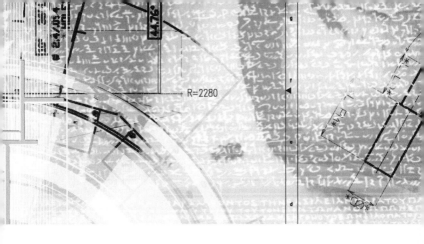

# PART ONE

# INTRODUCTION

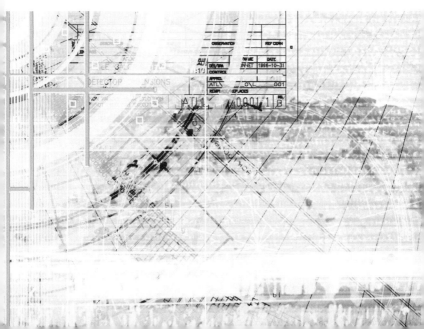

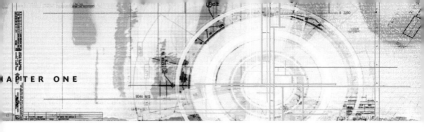

# CHAPTER ONE

# WAYS WE READ THE BIBLE

I think the Bible is a tough book to read. I say this as someone who loves to read. Next to my bed is a pile of eleven books—I just counted—that I want to read soon. Some are for fun, such as a collection of stories about Minnesota and the last of a series on the King Arthur legend. But they aren't *all* easy reading. In the pile I have a book by postmodern Italian novelist Umberto Eco (*Baudolino*), an ancient epic poem (*Beowulf*), and a philosophical poem (*Faust*). So you can see I'm not one to avoid difficult books.

But the Bible is unlike any other book I own. First of all, it's long—well over a thousand pages in most versions. Second, it was written over an extraordinarily long period of time, roughly two thousand years. Third, it's not written by just one person; dozens of people are responsible for this big book I hold in my hands. Actually, the word *biblia* in Greek means "books," and that's what the Bible really is—a compendium of many books, sixty-six to be exact.

Other aspects of this book make it unique. I don't own any other book that has little numbers preceding the sentences, nor do I have any other book that's bound in leather with my name embossed in gold ink on the front. And don't even get me started on those crinkly, see-through pages.

Ultimately the Bible is strange and unique for one reason: God gave it to us. That's what we as Christians believe: The Bible is inspired—breathed into being by the One who created the cosmos and who created you and me with the same breath. That's why we bind this book in leather and why medieval Christians bound their Bibles in jewels and precious metals. It's the reason some people change their tone of voice to sound more serious and reverent when reading the Bible out loud. That's why some people gasp if you accidentally drop a Bible on the floor or leave it on the roof of your car.

The Bibles we have today aren't covered with jewels, but we know they're something out of the ordinary even though they're made from the same trees as our school textbooks and favorite magazines. We know that when we hold a Bible in our hands, it's something special. It's unique. It's holy.

## THOSE WHO CAME BEFORE US

As you know, we're not the first Christians. Millions and millions of faithful Christ-followers have lived over the past two millennia, and many have tried to make sense of the same question that confronts us: How does one read this holy book?

Keep a couple of historical notes in mind when discovering how our forebears answered this question. The printing press wasn't invented until the fifteenth century. Until that time, Bibles were copied word for word by hand. Consequently, few Bibles existed, maybe one in a town. That means about three-fourths of the Christians who have lived never held Bibles in their hands. Instead, they heard the Bible being read or its stories being told around the hearth, and they saw events from the Bible depicted in stained glass and paintings in their churches and the homes of the wealthy.

It wasn't until the fourteenth century that the Bible was translated into languages other than Hebrew, Greek, and Latin. Many of our predecessors in the faith never read or heard the Bible in their own tongues, but only in a second or third language. If you've studied a foreign language, you know how this inherently changes the way you understand words and stories—or at least how hard you have to work to understand them.

With these considerations in mind, we can see how different our lives are today by having the Bible. I have over two dozen Bibles on my shelf, including over a dozen different translations. A bunch are study Bibles, meaning they have notes to help me understand what words, phrases, or whole paragraphs mean. Some people might say I'm far more fortunate than a Christian who lived during the Middle Ages because of the immediate availability of the Bible, but I'm not so sure. Instead, I wonder if I take it for granted, while many Christians who only saw the Bible once a week—when the priest carried it into worship, high over his head to show his reverence for God's Word—treasured it.

It was during this era that Saint Thomas Aquinas (A.D. 1224–1274), one of the greatest theologians who ever lived, thought about different meanings of the Bible. After consideration, he concluded that a passage of Scripture has four senses to it:

- *Literal:* the actual meaning of the words
- *Allegorical:* the figurative sense of the words
- *Moral:* the meaning of the words that spurs us to a moral, Christlike life
- *Anagogical* (from the Greek word for leading): the mostly hidden, mystical sense of the words, often pointing to some aspect of the afterlife or end times

Let's run the story of the Good Samaritan through this grid.

- *Literal:* Jesus tells a story about a man who was beaten by robbers but helped by a man from a different country, Samaria.
- *Allegorical:* The story is a parable, through which Jesus wants us to see that "neighbor" isn't limited to the person who lives next to us; it also means any person who inhabits this planet with us.
- *Moral:* Jesus wants us to emulate the Samaritan and help those in need, no matter their nationalities.
- *Anagogical:* The kingdom of heaven is a place of perfect healing and a place where earthly nationalities no longer matter.

When asked how the same text can have so many different senses, Aquinas answered by quoting Saint Gregory the Great (A.D. 540–604): "Holy Writ by the manner of its speech transcends every science, because in one and the same sentence, while it describes a fact, it reveals a mystery."[1] The Bible eclipses any human work of literature because it comes from the breath of God; and like a beautiful and sophisticated painting, a passage of Scripture has many meanings, all valid, and all placed there by him.

Aquinas's ideas about the senses of Scripture have been influential in the past centuries, and they are still. For instance, the *Catechism of the Catholic Church* (the major work of theological guidance for the world's one billion Roman Catholics) states that these four senses of the Bible should guide anyone who wishes to interpret its meanings.

## HOW WE READ TODAY

While Aquinas can give us some guidance, most of us today read in different ways than seven hundred years ago when books were scarce. To be honest, how I read the Bible is probably influenced more by how I read everyday material than by the methods of a medieval theologian.

We read on a daily basis for two reasons that occasionally overlap: information and entertainment. Every day, millions of us read newspapers; whether papers are delivered to our doorsteps or read online, we are primarily looking for information from them. We read about world affairs, the latest election results, what Congress is up to, the sports scores from last night, and the weather for the coming week. We read *Time* or *Newsweek* and school textbooks for informational purposes. In fact, you most likely picked up this book to be informed about a way to pray.

Meanwhile, we may be reading the comic section of the newspaper, *Sports Illustrated,* or our favorite blog site on the Internet for an entirely different reason: to be entertained.

While I hope this book is entertaining (at least enough to keep you reading!) and the author of your history textbook hopes for the same, that's not the primary reason either of us wrote nor the primary reason you're reading. However, that *is* why you might sneak *MAD* magazine into your backpack—to get a little humor and entertainment during your school day.

Let me persuade you that you have one other reason to read: life transformation. Life transformation is the reason we read great poetry or great novels. For example, the poems of Emily Dickinson are both informative (we learn about great poetry by reading it) and entertaining. Her poetry's greatest power is that she opens the world to us in new ways through it.

The same goes for *The Brothers Karamazov*, by Fyodor Dostoevsky, arguably the greatest novel ever written. It's a tale of the murder of a father by one of his three sons and the ensuing trial, but more than that, it's about a spiritual search, the search for God by the youngest son Ivan and his dialogue with the monk Zosima. Like Dickinson, Dostoevsky is able to portray the depths of the human soul in a rare and profound way, as well as the human love-hate relationship with the Father, both human and divine.

*The Brothers Karamazov* is not easy to read. While it's informative (depicting life in 1870s Russia) and entertaining (well written and, at points, extremely funny), those reasons alone probably aren't enough to get anyone through all 920 pages. We read a book like *The Brothers Karamazov* because, by its beauty and profundity, it changes us. We become better having read it. We better understand who we are as sinful human beings, and we better understand our deep need for relationships with God. Books the caliber of *The Brothers Karamazov* are life transforming because *we* are changed in the reading of *them*.

## HOW WE READ THE BIBLE

Ultimately, of course, life change is why we read the Bible, too. While it may be informative (teaching us about the history of Israel) and entertaining (a lot of those stories would make great movies!), Christians read the Bible because it changes us from the inside out. We believe that God has something to deliver to us via his inspired Word. God didn't have the Bible written over so many years because we needed a history—although we do; he inspired it so we would have a special revelation from him, a connection to him and his kingdom.

This realization should enliven us every time we crack open our Bibles, right? Unfortunately, in my experience, it doesn't. A lot of people agree with me—the Bible is difficult to read and tough to understand. An experience I had a couple years ago bears this out.

I lead a small group of high school seniors every year, so I met with the juniors in the spring and asked what they'd like to study the next fall. I figured they'd want to have an issues-oriented year—a couple weeks each on topics such as evolution, abortion, sex, homosexuality—because seniors usually want to talk about these topics to prepare for college.

To my surprise, these juniors said they'd like to study the Bible to get to know it better because they felt their biblical knowledge wasn't strong enough to handle the rigors of college.

I let them know I was surprised and went on to say that in my experience high school Bible studies that aren't issues-oriented or that don't follow a workbook rarely work because the students often don't do the reading.

"Yes!" they all cried in unison, almost breathing a sigh of relief that I might let them off the hook.

"I have the hardest time reading the Bible," Emily said. "My mind always wanders."

"I think it's really boring," agreed Craig.

Drew chimed in, "It's so hard to understand with all those names I can't pronounce and places I've never heard of."

The rest concurred. They considered the Bible almost unapproachable—big, daunting, and difficult. Indeed, this is why so many publishers have come out with books for high school students containing just the gospel of John or the book of Psalms. It's also why youth-group curriculum is often "hunt-and-fill"—search for one verse, fill in the blank, search for another verse, fill in the blank, and so on.

Students' near desperation and the hunt-and-fill curriculum are a result of a certain way we read the Bible. We most often read like miners. We go down into a dark mine shaft and pick away at a huge wall of words until we crack off a gem. That's what we take away from our time with the Bible.

Another metaphor I often use is of a scientist in a lab coat. That's how I was trained in seminary to study the Bible. I put a passage in a petri dish under a microscope and try to determine what it means by breaking it into its smallest parts. I know Hebrew and Greek, so I have the tools to crack it open. Unfortunately, all of this study hasn't made the Bible more alive to me. Instead, it has taught me to see the Bible as a problem to be solved.

This same dilemma is at the heart of the many study Bibles available for purchase today—each promises to help us through this challenging book with notes that explain the meanings of difficult words, cross-references that tell us where to find similar verses, and life-application boxes that interrupt the flow of the narrative to tell us how to apply biblical truth to our lives.

All of this is a result of the most common way of reading the Bible today: We consider it a problem to be solved or a nut to be cracked, as if God gave us a strange riddle wrapped in poetry, history, prophecy, gospel, epistle, and apocalypse that we have to solve to find out what it means to us today.

Another way of thinking about this perspective is to say that we stand over the Bible and attempt to interpret it.

This book is about something else. It's about an ancient way of putting ourselves under the Bible and letting *it* interpret *us* — lectio divina.

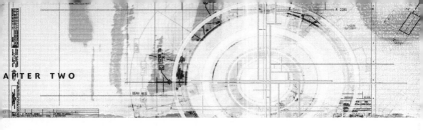

# CHAPTER TWO

# WHY PRAY THE BIBLE?

I think prayer is difficult. I know, it sounds like I'm repeating myself. First I said that reading the Bible is tough, and now I'm saying the same thing about prayer. Prayer and the Bible— those are the two basics of the Christian faith, and I'm admitting that they're both hard for me. Sorry if you think I'm a wimp, but I'm being honest about my own experience.

This might not be true for you, because I've met lots of people for whom prayer comes quite naturally. Those people are in almost constant contact with God, a continual conversation with their Creator. In the history of the church, plenty of saints seem to have prayed this way. Julian of Norwich, a teenage girl in England, actually had herself locked in a room so that nothing would interrupt her ongoing prayers to and revelations from God. And the anonymous Russian wayfarer who wrote *The Way of a Pilgrim* prayed the Jesus Prayer— "Lord Jesus Christ, Son of God, have mercy on me, a sinner"—throughout his adult life twelve thousand times each day![2] These are people who took the apostle Paul's exhortation to pray all the time (see 1 Thessalonians 5:17) seriously!

I'm just here to tell you that has not been my experience during prayer, which is characterized by a wandering mind and difficulty concentrating. I've tried it all: first thing in the morning, last thing in the evening, standing, sitting, kneeling, and everyone's favorite, lying in bed. I've tried praying while I'm driving the car and praying while I take a walk. I've prayed alone, with my wife Julie, and with our kids.

I've tried sure-fire models of prayer such as A.C.T.S. (adoration, confession, thanksgiving, supplication). They've all worked, at least for a short time. The problem, as you may know, is that prayer takes a certain amount of self-discipline. We've got to set aside the time and find a place conducive to prayer. (I think this is why prayer-while-driving has never worked for me.)

One of the necessities of focused prayer is to commit it to a particular time and place every day. For me, it's first thing in the morning right now. I have two small children, and I have a great time with God after they wake up, as we talk about God and pray together.

But having two wide-awake toddlers is not particularly conducive to a quiet time alone with Jesus, so I've been getting up before they do (around 5 A.M.) to pray and write. No one likes to get up at five in the morning, but that has become part of my daily spiritual routine. As a result, I've had some of the most fruitful and fulfilling prayer times in my life.

We can't always wing it with prayer. Of course, we can pray anytime about anything, and we should stay in constant contact with God, but in order to hear from God and give him the focus he deserves, a special time is important. This "hearing from God" is a tricky subject. Some people "hear" from God all the time, while others of us long desperately for a word of direction from the Lord. In this book, I am not writing about actually hearing God's voice through our physical ears (although that may happen), but about being quiet enough and focused enough on God's Word for him to move our spirits and to give us some sense of his will for us.

*Enough already!* you may be thinking.

Making time for God is the first big step, and it's not an easy one to take. It requires an extraordinary amount of discipline, more than is usually asked of us. And yet taking time to spend with God and his Word is primary to the practice of lectio divina.

Once you've carved out some regular time for God and committed to it (even if you're falling down and picking yourself up time and again), the question remains: What do we do with our prayer time? What method of prayer should we use? When we look at examples in the Bible, true prayer seems to be conversation with God. Think of Moses or David or Jesus. However, I've mostly fallen into the trap of asking, asking, asking, talking, talking, talking. Modern Christian prayer may be most characterized as us talking and initiating while God listens and responds. Sometimes God might be shouting — or whispering — to us, "That's enough! Now you sit there and listen to me for a while."

The reasons for our talkativeness in prayer are obvious enough. To begin with, God doesn't talk as we do. God, while present with us at all times, has neither a physical presence that we can see nor vocal cords to articulate those things he wants us to hear. Neither does God write us E-mails. Our relationship with him is unlike any other relationship we have. If friends or family members have something to say to me, they'll say it, even if they have to interrupt me. That's not how God works.

Another reason for our loquacious prayer lives is that we've heard lots of people (often in church) give long, flowery speeches to or about God that they call prayer. Some of us feel a lot of pressure, thinking the only way to speak to God is with big, theological-sounding words.

Have you ever noticed how some prayers are cluttered with the words *um, uh,* and, the bane of Christian prayer, *just* (as in, "O Lord, we just ask that you would . . . ")? We clutter our prayers with these verbal tics to fill space, spewing an endless string of words before God's throne.

Another reason we do so much talking in our prayers is our fear of silence. Our lives are filled with noise, often from the time the alarm goes off in the morning until our favorite CD lulls us to sleep at night. We're surrounded by sound. Without a doubt, we live in the noisiest, most media- and technology-saturated society ever. Most of the high school students in my church are constantly bombarded by noise, even doing their homework with TVs or radios playing and instant messaging services delivering new E-mails at a second's notice.

Noise inhibiting our prayers is an age-old problem. In the fourth and fifth centuries, the desert fathers and mothers thought that Jerusalem was too loud to be conducive to prayer, so they moved out of the city and dwelt in caves in the wilderness. Today disconnecting from noise means turning off cell phones, pagers, computers, TVs, stereos, and other conveniences. Only then are we truly ready to be receptive to what God has to say.

## DIVINE REVELATION (OR HOW GOD SPEAKS)

Where do we turn when we want to hear what God has to say to us? The Bible!

Of course, God speaks to us in many ways. Sometimes he speaks to us through friends. God has a long history of moving through the Spirit in community. I've had to make several big decisions during my lifetime, one recently. I took this decision to two small groups I participate in. I asked all the members of the two groups to pray over the course of six months, asking God for guidance. After six months, everyone in both groups (twenty people in all) agreed about what I should do. At the beginning of the process, I prayed to God that he would work through the communities to guide me, so when both groups had consensus, I took it on faith that God had spoken to me through this process.

You may also hear from God in nature or in a place that's particularly special to you. Often it takes getting away from our usual surroundings to hear his voice. For many people, spending time in his creation is how this best occurs. My family owns some forested property in northern Minnesota, and I know that when I walk alone through those woods, I often achieve an intense communion with God and some clarity about otherwise muddy areas of my life.

Some people (though I'm not one of them) have great success at "listening prayer," basically prayers of silence while sitting and waiting for God to speak. The pray-er may ask God a question and then wait and listen until God answers it. Often the pray-er's spirit is moved by God's Spirit toward an answer or she perhaps even hears a voice with an answer or a blessing.

All these ways of hearing from God work some or even most of the time. The problem with all of them is that they're fallible. You might not be receiving *God's* revelation; your impression might simply be wrong. Sure, I think God spoke to me through my two small-group communities, but maybe people with their own agendas happened to agree about my future. The clarity I receive during a walk in the woods might be of my own imagination, not anything from God. Even proponents of listening prayer admit they have no way of knowing which voices are God's and which come from other sources.

As human beings, we have only one infallible revelation from God: the Bible. *Infallible* means the Bible will not lead us into error or sin when it's read by a faithful person, one who's following Christ, one who takes seriously the context in which the verse or passage was written. So, although God is revealed to us in nature (which he created) and in other people (who are made in his image), the Bible is where we can ultimately and confidently turn to hear from God.

## IT'S ALIVE!

A friend of mine calls the Bible "the nonfiction storybook of God's interaction with humankind." Some of us may get hung up on the word *storybook*, thinking it implies a lack of truth or historicity. But the Bible *is* a collection of stories, some from the ancient past of Israel and some from the more recent past of Jesus and his early followers. The stories are very much true and very much alive.

The aliveness of the Bible and the stories within it are what sets Christian Scripture apart from any other book you can buy. Remember my analogy of reading the Bible like a scientist looking through a microscope? Another way to understand that way of reading the Bible is like dissecting an animal in science class. I can remember getting my formaldehyde-soaked baby pig in tenth-grade biology class. Mainly I remember the smell! My lab partners and I named him Porky. Porky was dead, of course. The only way to dissect something is to kill it first.

This is what we often do to the Bible when we get hung up on a word or a phrase or a verse. We deaden the liveliness of the book God has given us when we spend more time reading the notes in our study Bibles than we spend reading the actual text. When we try to freeze the Bible in a certain time period, it becomes like an ancient relic soaked in embalming fluid.

That way of reading the Bible—deadening and then dissecting it—stands in contradiction to the way Christians have always understood our sacred book. John Robinson (A.D. 1575–1625) was the pastor of the Pilgrims before they left on the *Mayflower* for the New World. His famous saying summarizes a different way of approaching Scripture: "There is yet more light and truth to break forth from God's Holy Word."[3] In other words, God has new things to say to us through the Bible today. Scripture is not static. It's not like a history textbook that simply records events from long ago. Instead it's living and active and has the ability to constantly transform the lives of people.

You might think "the Bible is living" is a weird idea. You might have a Bible near you right now. Look at it. It sits there, inanimate, made of dead trees and maybe bound with the hide of a dead cow. That doesn't seem living in any way. The Bible lives in another sense: Because it's God-breathed, it has the ability to breathe God's Spirit into us. Think of it this way: The belief of Christ-followers is that, though the Bible is done being written, it's not done writing. The Bible writes its truths on our hearts, speaking its words constantly into new situations, new times, and new cultures. God's Spirit is alive and well and enables us to read the Bible in faith. No other book can make that claim.

## BUT HOW?

All that may make sense, but it leads us to a big question: How do we receive God's Spirit when we read the Bible? How can we allow ourselves to be led by the Spirit as we read the Word? The answer may be by praying the Bible—that is, using the words of Scripture as your prayer, either by yourself or with the members of your prayer or Bible study group. After praying words of Scripture, stop to listen, to hear what God has to say to you in those infallible words. Lectio divina is a way of doing just that; and it's one good reason Christians have been doing lectio divina for over fifteen hundred years.

# CHAPTER THREE

# WHERE DID LECTIO DIVINA
## COME FROM?

Because you haven't heard anyone speak Latin lately, you may have guessed that lectio divina is ancient, and indeed it is. But another way of praying Scripture even predates Christianity.

The prayer book right in the middle of the Bible is the book of Psalms. It's guided the prayer life of God's followers for four thousand years. The 150 psalms contained in this book have been said and often sung by Jews and Christians for all that time as well. Indeed, as we will see later, the psalms make some of the best material for lectio divina.

The psalmist declares, "Seven times each day I stop and shout praises for the way you keep everything running right" (Psalm 119:164). We don't know when those seven times a day were, but we can assume that many of the psalms were the praises the psalmist shouted. The psalms make up a body of prayers that express the gamut of human emotions, from joy to desperation, from security to fear. The psalms are, in many ways, the most personal, emotional, and immediate prayers available to us, which is why they've been so popular for thousands of years.

Jesus quoted and referred to several psalms.[4] We can safely assume he knew them and prayed them often because they were the basis of Hebrew prayer in his day. We also know that Jesus often withdrew from the crowds of people who surrounded him in order to pray to and with his Father. I write "to and with" because we get the impression when reading about Jesus' moments of prayer that he was not only talking *to* God but that he was also hearing *from* God. Prayer was an interaction between the two, as we can see by the dramatic results. On the Mount of Transfiguration, Jesus' prayer was so intense that "the appearance of his face changed and his clothes became blinding white" (Luke 9:29), and Moses and Elijah showed up to talk with him. At a later point, while praying in the Garden of Gethsemane, "he plunged into an agonizing sorrow" (Matthew 26:37).

Reactions like these don't happen during one-way prayer. Jesus must have been talking *and* listening—a two-way conversation. That's a call-and-response pattern similar to what we see in many of the psalms. Take Psalm 6, for instance. The psalmist cries out to God,

> *Can't you see I'm black and blue,*
> *    beat up badly in bones and soul?*
> *God, how long will it take*
> *    for you to let up?* (verses 2-3)

He exclaims that his bed is wet with tears. He has been weeping, waiting for God to respond. Suddenly a response comes, and the psalmist cries out,

> Get out of here, you Devil's crew:
>> at last God has heard my sobs.
> My requests have all been granted,
>> my prayers are answered. (verses 8-9)

The same type of sudden reversal happens in a lot of psalms. Someone is crying and weeping and in despair at God's absence, when God suddenly arrives on the scene, the Enemy is defeated, and the psalmist sings God's praises. This kind of change can only take place in conversation (as opposed to monologue). Like Jesus, the psalmist is both talking and listening. He's being quiet enough to hear God's response after he calls out.

## LISTENING TO THE HOLY SPIRIT IN CAVES

Listening is the key to lectio divina. As we've already examined, listening isn't something human beings do all that well. We may think difficulty in being able to listen is mainly a problem of our noisy age, but it's not. Only a couple hundred years after Jesus lived, devout men and women who were trying to prayerfully listen to God felt that the cities they were living in were too noisy. So they moved out of cities such as Jerusalem and Athens, taking residence in caves and on the sides of mountains.

Between the fourth and fourteenth centuries, hundreds of these pray-ers withdrew to caves in the wilderness, and they became known as the desert fathers and mothers. The fame of their great piety and prayer spread, and over that millennium, thousands of pilgrims traveled to see the desert dwellers and learn from them. Rufinus was a young pilgrim who met with many of the desert fathers, and he wrote of his experience: "This is the utter desert where each monk remains alone in his cell. . . . There is a huge silence and a great quiet here."[5]

Although they weren't bound by a single way for life, some patterns did emerge in the prayer lives of the desert fathers and mothers. Their lives were bound by a list of virtues, which Gregory of Sinai (A.D. 1296–1359) lists as "fasting, abstinence, vigil, patience, courage, silence, prayer, not talking, tears, humility, which generate and preserve one another."[6] Isn't it interesting that he would list both "silence" and "not talking"? He's driving home the point that being quiet by not speaking or doing anything to create noise is one of the keys to hearing from God.

Those who lived in the desert did hear from God, often through lectio divina. They didn't have copies of the Bible to read, but they had committed large portions of Scripture to memory, and they meditated on different passages, letting God speak to them through his Word.

## MEANWHILE, ACROSS THE MEDITERRANEAN . . .

Although the desert fathers and mothers were highly disciplined in their spiritual lives, no specific organization was pulling them all together. Each was on his or her own. Events were transpiring differently across the Mediterranean Sea in Europe. There, a young man named Benedict was born in Nursia, Italy, around A.D. 480. His parents sent him to school in Rome, but much like his colleagues in the East, Benedict was disgusted with the sin and noise that he found in that city. (At the time, Rome was nearing the end of its run as the capital of the world, so it was disintegrating.)

Benedict left Rome and took up residence outside of Subiaco, a little village in the Italian hills. Having seen his classmates in Rome fall victim to sins of all kinds, he decided the way to a true relationship with God was through penitential solitude. He lived in a cave for three years, fasting and praying in silence. A choice like this might seem crazy to us today; it seemed just as crazy back then. Although the people who occasionally left food for him kept his location secret, word began to spread about this hermit and his cave, and others came to visit him and learn from him.

Gradually, a small group of young men decided they wanted to join with Benedict in his monastic life. The first group of men who joined him grew so weary of his rigorous way of life that they tried to poison him! Through a miracle, the pitcher containing the poison shattered just as he was about to drink it.

Benedict returned to a solitary life, but eventually another group of monks convinced him to become their leader (their *abbot*, meaning "father"). They left Subiaco and built a monastery on Monte Cassino. As their number increased, Benedict sent them to start new monasteries, each with twelve monks and an abbot.

While it was every monk for himself in the caves of the East, the Benedictine monks had a structure and organization that tied them together. Around 540, Benedict wrote *The Rule* (now known as *The Rule of Saint Benedict*). *The Rule* outlines life in a monastery, from the seven worship services every day to how and when to do the dishes, from what buildings to construct to disciplining a brother who oversleeps. It defines a rigorous standard and continues to govern the life of most Roman Catholic monks today.

Three activities dominate the life of a Benedictine monk: prayer, work, and lectio divina. Although most of the day in a Benedictine monastery is quiet, and all idle talk is forbidden, lectio divina is frequent. Reading takes place in the monks' cells, in common areas, and while the brothers are eating.

Here is what Benedict wrote in *The Rule* about lectio divina: "Idleness is an enemy of the soul. Therefore, the brothers should be occupied according to schedule in either manual labor or holy reading." He goes on to write at length about how a monk should read for much of the day. In the summer, monks read from 10 A.M. until noon; in the winter, from waking (4 A.M.!) until 8 A.M.; and in the spring, from waking until 9 A.M. And they read at night, too.

If you think Benedict may not have been serious about this, he says that a couple of the older brothers should be chosen to oversee the reading periods. "They will check that no one is slothful, lazy or gossiping, profiting himself and disturbing others."[7] This may seem particularly harsh or strict, but the instructions were, after all, for those becoming monks.

For the past fifteen hundred years, monks of the strict observance—monasteries that closely follow *The Rule*—have spent much of their days reading. Monasteries have special reading rooms and often have impressive libraries. In the Dark

Ages, monasteries preserved many of the world's greatest pieces of literature by protecting and copying books in their libraries. Between reading, copying books, and hearing the Bible read in worship and at meals (conversation is not allowed at meals), much of a monk's day is spent meditating on the Word of God.

Thomas Keating is a Catholic priest in Massachusetts who has been influential in the recovery of ancient prayer practices. He notes that classic lectio divina, as practiced by most monks from A.D. 500 to 1000, didn't have a set form. As a monk read or heard Scripture, his mind alternated between reading, meditation, contemplation, and prayer, in no particular order.[8] While this may be fine for a monk who spends his whole life steeped in lectio divina, I suggest we look to the format explained by a monk in the Middle Ages.

## FOLLOWING GUIGO II

Though dates differ, Guigo II lived from about A.D. 1115 to 1198. His official title was the Ninth Prior of the Grand Chartreuse of Carthusians. That's a mouthful. Here's what it means: The Carthusians are an order of monks who are particularly strict (for example, they wake up every night at 11:45 P.M. and pray for three hours!). The headquarters of their order is the Grand Chartreuse (Charterhouse), which is just outside of Grenoble, France. The prior is the leader of the Charterhouse and, therefore, of all Carthusians around the world. Guigo II was the ninth monk to lead the order.

In about 1150, Guigo II wrote *The Ladder of Monastics* (also known as *The Ladder of Four Rungs*). He compares the way monks pray and seek God to the ladder that Jacob saw climbing to heaven at Bethel (see Genesis 28:11-19). Guigo begins his book by telling about how all this occurred to him while he was working in the garden:

> *One day I was engaged in physical work with my hands and I began to think about the spiritual tasks we humans have. While I was thinking, four spiritual steps came to mind: reading (lectio), meditation (meditatio), prayer (oratio), and contemplation (contemplatio). This is the ladder of monastics by which they are lifted up from the earth into heaven. There are only a few distinct steps, but the distance covered is beyond measure and belief since the lower part is fixed on the earth and its top passes through the clouds to lay bare the secrets of heaven.*[9]

While earlier Christians prayed lectio divina in something of a "web" form, jumping in and jumping out of steps in any order they chose, Guigo changed the metaphor to that of a ladder.

With that hierarchical model, lectio divina has a specific starting point and ending point. We begin, he writes, on earth, reading God's Word. Then we climb the rungs of meditation and prayer, finally arriving in the clouds of heaven in contemplation.

Guigo's format is the one we're going to follow in this book. Maybe I'm a slave to formulas or maybe I'm not as good at lectio divina as I ought to be, but I find his metaphor helpful. You may graduate to a more fluid method of praying Scripture, and I'm sure even Guigo would say we aren't bound to his formulation. But the linear structure of a ladder is a good starting point to learn lectio divina.

In part 2, we'll look at each step of lectio divina. You'll want to leave behind what you think you already know about reading and prayer and be ready to consider new ideas. You might be surprised by the wonderful complexities of meditation and contemplation.

Remember, lectio divina is about one thing: developing an intimate relationship with God by praying the Scripture he gave us. Just as Guigo pointed out, every one of us who follows Christ wants to experience heaven, even for a moment, because it reminds us of why we slog through the difficulties of life on earth. Lectio divina may help you climb into God's lap for a few moments today.

# PART TWO

# THE STEPS OF LECTIO DIVINA

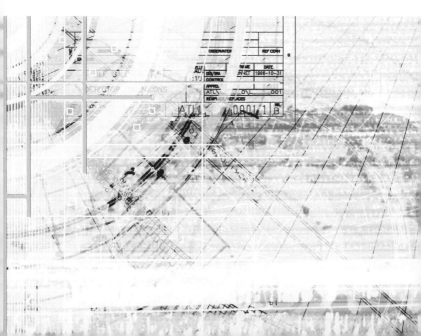

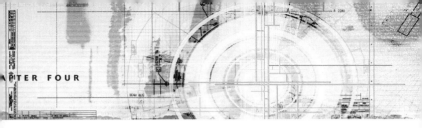

# LECTIO

My wife Julie gave me a wonderful Christmas gift recently—a subscription to the Sunday edition of the *New York Times*. The tag line of the *Times* is, "All the News That's Fit to Print." It's also known as the "paper of record" in the United States, which means it's generally considered the most important newspaper published in the country (probably in the world), although people at the *Washington Post* and the *Times* of London might heartily disagree with that.

I love the Sunday *Times!* It's filled with some of the best writing of the world's journalists, not to mention the editorials and the columns. It also contains the film and theater reviews and a whole separate section on books. The *Times* has only a few pictures and no comics; in that way it seems old-fashioned. Still, it has a sophisticated feel, and when I read it, I can almost imagine for a few moments that I live in a studio apartment in SoHo and have tickets for a Broadway show lying on the table by the door.

The Sunday *Times* is huge! It usually takes me all week to read it. I'll often read the front section on Sunday, work my way through the other sections all week, and finally get to the book reviews on Saturday, finishing just in time to find the next edition on my front step on Sunday morning.

I would rather sit down with a cup of coffee for three or four hours on Sunday afternoon to read the whole thing all at once—but that's not possible because of two words: *Tanner* and *Lily*. Those are our kids. Currently, Tanner is two and Lily is one. They're full of life! So when they're awake, they need me to be available for reading stories, wrestling on the floor, kissing boo-boos, and changing dirty diapers. As much as I'd like to read the *Times*, when Tanner and Lily are awake, the paper is put away. After they go down for naps or for the evening, Julie and I need to have some adult talk or wash dishes or throw in a load of laundry—or many times we collapse into bed ourselves.

So the *Times* gets read here and there, piece by piece, section by section. Once I started reading the same article four times, and each time I was interrupted. I put the paper down, kissed a boo-boo, played with the kids, and then searched high and low for the newspaper to start reading again.

The way I read the Sunday *Times* is not classified as restful reading. Imagine the exact opposite of the way I read the *Times*. That's how lectio divina begins.

## TUNA TARTARE OR HOT DOGS

A lot of the reading you do probably happens like my reading of the *New York Times*. You frantically read a book for literature or English class so you can write a two-page synopsis due in the morning. Or you have to read the paper or a magazine for a current events oral report. Or maybe you've got to read two chapters of the Bible before your small group meets tonight (in which case, you'd better put down this book and get crackin'!).

The reading called for in lectio divina, however, is similar to our everyday reading only in that each uses words and eyeballs. Otherwise they're completely different. Where reading for school is hurried, lectio is slow. Where reading a magazine is superficial, lectio is deep. Where reading a novel is for entertainment, lectio is for communing with God. Where our usual Bible study is so we'll know more *about* God, lectio is so we'll hear more *from* God.

Lectio reading is slow, quiet, and deep. At first I found lectio to be painfully slow. During high school, college, and graduate school, I became better and better at reading more words in less time — something like my method for a hot dog–eating contest — I needed to see how fast I could read and still do it well enough to regurgitate the information on a test or a paper in a limited amount of time.

Lectio isn't a hot dog–eating contest. It's an elegant banquet.

For those of us used to snarfing hot dogs, a refined cuisine is hard to get used to. For one thing, the portions are quite small and are meant to be eaten slowly, every bite a savory experience. The ingredients are expensive, and the chef has carefully blended them in perfect combination.

One of the best meals I've ever had was in an upscale restaurant in New York City. My entrée was called the DB Burger, the signature dish of the menu. The description read, "Sirloin burger filled with braised short ribs, *foie gras*, and black truffles served on a Parmesan bun with *pommes soufflées*." That's quite a hamburger, and it cost $29!

The most incredible taste of that night wasn't burger, though. Compliments of the house (because our table wasn't ready when we arrived), my brothers and I were given an appetizer of tuna tartare: raw, ground tuna. I realize that sounds gross to most people. Each of us was given a small spoon with a little tuna on it. That was it. Merely a taste, but what a taste! The flavor exploded in my mouth. It was unlike anything I had ever tasted. If I close my eyes, I can almost taste it now.

That's what lectio divina's first step, reading, is like. It's that slow, that savory, and that explosive.

## SETTING THE MOOD

One of the keys to any contemplative prayer experience is making sure the pray-er and the atmosphere are conducive to contemplation. Here are some of the fundamentals for lectio divina.

### The Room

It's important that the physical place you choose to pray using the lectio divina method is quiet. Although some people like to have chant or other soft music in the background to drown out distracting noise, complete silence is best. One of the goals of lectio divina is to become totally absorbed in the words of God, which is difficult to achieve with distractions of any kind. For this reason, I favor practicing lectio divina indoors initially. Once you've become experienced in this style of prayer, you can try it outside.

### The Chair

In order to pray, you'll want to find a posture that's somewhere between comfortable and uncomfortable. The most important aspect of your posture is that your spine is straight. No slouching! (Do I sound like your mother?) Contemplative prayer is often aided by sitting in a firm chair—no lying on a couch or bed—with both feet firmly on the ground; hands palms up, one on either leg; head either looking straight ahead or with the chin on the chest.

Some people prefer kneeling, especially because it embodies a spirit of humility before God. Kneeling takes some getting used to, so try putting a pillow on your heels to sit on at first. Whatever posture you choose, it should be comfortable enough not to distract you and uncomfortable enough to keep you awake and attentive.

### The Tummy

Similarly, find a middle ground between hungry and full for lectio divina. Too hungry and you'll be distracted by your stomach; too full and you're likely to become sleepy. If you don't pray lectio divina first thing in the morning (which I'll suggest in a moment), try it midway between meals, so your tummy isn't a distracting factor.

### The Eyes

The desert fathers, who lived in caves, said that dawn and dusk are most conducive to contemplative prayer. They taught their followers that a cave (for us, a room) should be neither full of light nor totally dark. They directed pray-ers to have their eyes partly open. The thinking is that if your eyes are wide open, you're more likely to be distracted by something moving past you or an object on the wall or in the room, but if your eyes are completely closed, your imagination produces images and daydreams.

Of course, your eyes have to be open for the reading portion of lectio divina, and the room has to be bright enough to read the words, but you might want to try keeping your eyes half-open to see if it works for you.

### The Time

I like to pray first thing in the morning. Not only are my kids still in bed, but I'm also attentive at 5 A.M., especially after a cup of coffee. Getting up that early is a discipline. I just don't get up that early by nature. I've had to train my body to become used to that, and I have to make sure I get to bed around 10 P.M. to be able to rise that early. You may not have kids, but you may have to get up as early as I do to pray through lectio divina and still get to school or your job or your activities on time.

If you're not a morning person, you'll have to find a time of day that works for you. You may find that first thing in the morning doesn't work because you get sidetracked by everything you have to do that day, or maybe you'll have a harder time praying at night because you can't tear yourself away from the events of the day easily.

The best thing is to experiment. Try a variety of times to see what works best for you.

Another time aspect to consider is how long to stay in each

of the four stages. There's no right way to do it. You'll see in the back of this book a dozen passages along with some suggested amounts of time, but these are just guidelines. When you're doing lectio divina alone, you decide how long to rest in each step.

A lectio divina group meets at a Catholic church downtown in my city every Saturday morning. Because the leader doesn't want even the sound of her voice to interrupt our prayer, she softly rings a bell to signal a move from one step to another. You can experience the same result by setting a clock that has multiple alarms or by setting a watch that has a countdown function. When you hear the alarm, you move into the next step of lectio divina. Make sure to use an alarm that has a gentle ring, so you aren't jarred by it.

As you become more experienced with lectio divina, you'll find you move naturally from one stage to the next without external cues. You'll move whenever the time is right. As you become more versed in this style of prayer, let God move you however and wherever he wants to move you.

## PICKING THE PASSAGE

Because the entire Bible is inspired by God, it's all worthy of being prayed by way of lectio divina, but some parts are easier to pray than others. A good place to begin is with passages that naturally lend themselves to devotional reading. In lectio divina you want to be spiritually swept out of this world and into God's heaven, so a good place to begin is in the Psalms.

You won't need more than a few verses. The point in lectio divina is not to imbibe large portions of Scripture, but to have a small taste that you can sit with for an extended period of time. Psalm 117 is the perfect starting length.

> *Praise God, everybody!*
> *Applaud God, all people!*
> *His love has taken over our lives;*
> *God's faithful ways are eternal.*
> *Hallelujah!*

The Old Testament books of the prophets are also full of poetry and song, which are excellent for lectio divina.

A good place to begin in the New Testament is in the letters of John, for instance, 1 John 4:7-8:

> *My beloved friends, let us continue to love each other*
> *since love comes from God. Everyone who loves is*
> *born of God and experiences a relationship with God.*
> *The person who refuses to love doesn't know the first*

> *thing about God, because God is love — so you can't*
> *know him if you don't love.*

Next, you can move into the Gospels to pray one of Jesus' parables or try a portion of the Sermon on the Mount, found in Matthew 5–7.

At first you should stay away from your favorite verses and stories, because you may find it difficult to come to them clean — that is, without presuppositions. But after you've had some experience with lectio divina, go to a passage that you underlined or highlighted in your Bible years ago. Come to it fresh, as though you're reading it for the first time. And then watch out for the new ideas God can teach you from an old, familiar passage.

Another way to choose a passage is to use a lectionary (see *lectio* in that word?), a list of Scripture passages that follows the church calendar and repeats every three years. For every Sunday, the lectionary identifies a psalm, an Old Testament reading, a New Testament reading, and a Gospel lesson. You can find lectionaries in books and on the Internet. You can also use the *Daily Office*, similarly published in books and on the Internet, which has Scripture for every day using a two-year cycle.[10]

There are two good reasons to use a lectionary: (1) You're

often reading passages that coincide with the seasons of the year (Advent, Christmas, Lent, Easter); and (2) the text is chosen for you, so you won't be tempted to pick a passage where you "know" what God might say to you.

However you choose to pick your verses, use some you're familiar with and discover new ones. Experiment with passages throughout the Bible and of different lengths. You'll fall in love with God's Word in a whole new way.

## RESTFUL READING

Now that you're sitting comfortably and you've chosen your passage, it's time to read. There's no secret formula to the first step of lectio divina. Just read the passage slowly and repeatedly. Let it sink in. Read it out loud, and read it silently. Become familiar with the rhythms of the text, its ebbs and flows.

Your mind may wander to the matters of the day. Just return to your reading. Don't beat yourself up for having wandering thoughts. It happens to everyone. Try not to be abrupt during your move back into reading. Be gentle and gradual. Let the words of the text be your response to any distractions, repelling the distraction before it sidetracks you completely.

You won't find a rule anywhere about how many times you should read the passage. Maybe five times, maybe fifteen. It depends on how many times seem right to you. Focus only on the words, phrases, and sentences. Don't try to figure out what they mean. Don't try to imagine the context in which they were written. And when you're experienced at lectio divina, be sure to not move into meditation prematurely.

Let your reading be restful and unhurried. God's Word is his gift to you. It's a blessing—so let it bless you. Experience it; don't intellectualize it. Let the experience of reading God's Word be just that for you—an experience of reading God's Word.

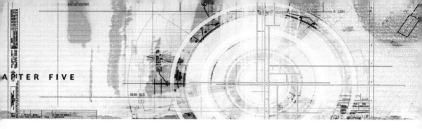

# CHAPTER FIVE

# MEDITATIO

When you hear the word *meditation* you might think of a Buddhist monk, head shaved, wrapped in colorful robes, surrounded by candles, sitting with his hands on his knees, chanting, "Ommmmm." Or maybe you imagine a yoga instructor sitting cross-legged in front of a yoga class. You might even think of NBA coach Phil Jackson, a self-proclaimed "Buddhist Christian," preparing for a basketball game.

Most of our popular images of meditation are linked to Eastern religions, particularly Buddhism and Hinduism. But the tradition of meditation in Christianity goes back over fifteen hundred years. Early Christians used the word *meditate* to mean memorizing Scripture. Believers memorized a passage (no verse numbers then) in the morning, and then meditated on it all day. We can learn something about meditation by going back even further—into the Old Testament.

## GNAW THAT BONE!

Depending on what version of the Bible you use, the word *meditate* appears about fifteen times in the Old Testament. (It's not used at all in the New Testament.) Fourteen of the Old Testament uses are in the Psalms, six in Psalm 119.

The one reference to *meditate* not in a psalm is a famous line from the opening of the book of Joshua. Moses has just died, and God speaks to Joshua, who will be leading the people of Israel into their Promised Land:

> "Moses my servant is dead. Get going. Cross this Jordan River, you and all the people. Cross to the country I'm giving to the People of Israel. . . . I'll be with you. I won't give up on you; I won't leave you. Strength! Courage! . . . Make sure you carry out The Revelation that Moses commanded you, every bit of it. Don't get off track, either left or right, so as to make sure you get to where you're going. And don't for a minute let this Book of The Revelation be out of mind. Ponder and meditate on it day and night, making sure you practice everything written in it. Then you'll get where you're going; then you'll succeed."
> (Joshua 1:2-8)

We can learn some things about the concept of meditation from this passage. To meditate means to keep something in mind—in fact, to keep it in the front of your mind. God tells Joshua that his success at leading the people into Canaan is tied to his meditation on the books of Moses (commonly understood to be Genesis, Exodus, Leviticus, Numbers, and Deuteronomy).

Meditation and practice are linked. "Ponder and meditate on it day and night, making sure you practice everything written in it." God doesn't want Joshua to merely think about his Word. He also wants Joshua to put it into practice. Meditating on God's Word and living God's Word are, God says to Joshua, inextricably tied together.

Eugene Peterson translated *The Message*, and he writes that the Hebrew word for *meditate* is *hagah*, which can also be translated "growl" or "chew." For instance, that's the word used in Isaiah's prophecy: "Like a lion, king of the beasts, that gnaws and chews and worries its prey" (Isaiah 31:4). The kind of meditation that God calls Joshua to, and the kind of meditation that the psalmist calls all of us to, is more like a dog chewing a bone, or a lion working over a carcass, than what we usually think of as meditation. Peterson writes,

> *"Meditate" is far too tame a word for what is being*
> *signified. "Meditate" seems more suited to what I do*
> *in a chapel on my knees with a candle burning on*
> *the altar. Or my wife sitting in a rose garden with*

> the Bible open in her lap. But when Isaiah's lion and
> my dog meditated, they chewed and swallowed,
> using teeth and tongue, stomach and intestines.[11]

The opening of the first psalm is usually translated,

> Happy are those who do not follow the advice of the
> wicked,
>> or take the path that sinners tread,
>> or sit in the seat of scoffers;
> but their delight is in the law of the Lord,
>> and on his law they meditate day and night.
> (verses 1-2, NRSV, emphasis added)

In *The Message*, Peterson translates it as,

> How well God must like you —
>> you don't hang out at Sin Saloon,
>> you don't slink along Dead-End Road,
>> you don't go to Smart-Mouth College.
> Instead you thrill to GOD's Word,
>> you chew on Scripture day and night.
> (verses 1-2, emphasis added)

## AN ACTIVE MIND

Peterson is emphasizing an enduring understanding among God's people: Meditation is an active exercise. Our thought of a Buddhist monk or a Hindu yogi sitting cross-legged and emptying his mind through meditation stands at odds with the Christian concept of meditation. Meditation for Christians demands an engaged, active mind. This is meditatio, the second step of lectio divina.

If lectio (reading) can be compared to tasting food, then meditatio is like chewing. It's working an idea over in your mind, just as you chew food in your mouth before you swallow it. Ignatius of Loyola (1491–1556) wrote at length about meditation. He may be the all-time Christian expert on meditation. In the *Spiritual Exercises*, he offers excellent ideas for Christians to actively engage their minds with the text of Scripture by using imagination to enter the biblical scene.

In lectio divina, the reading of a passage leads to meditation. As you read the text repeatedly, chances are that a certain word or phrase will become most notable to you. It will stand out and rise above the other words. The faith with which we pray lectio divina is that God has a word for us, that God will speak to us personally through Scripture. With that in mind, we pay attention to the word or phrase that grabs hold of us during the reading.

As we gently let go of the reading, we take up meditation. We let all the other words fall aside, and we focus in on that word or phrase that has become primary.

Say I've chosen Psalm 1:1-2 for my lectio. After reading the passage slowly several times, the word *thrill* has grabbed my attention—or I should say, God has brought *thrill* to my attention.

Having received that word, I stop reading. My mind's eye, instead of focusing on the printed words on the page, looks inward, inside me. I start to chew on *thrill*. I work it over in my mind, silently thinking the word over and over: *thrill* . . . *thrill* . . . *thrill*. What is the word causing me to feel? What is it causing me to think?

Another metaphor for meditation, in addition to chewing, is a shining light. I look at *thrill* from different angles, shining a spotlight on it from every side. I flip it over, upside down, inside out. What does *thrill* mean? When I shine a bright light on the word, when I take a close look at it in my mind's eye, what do I see?

## IN HARMONY WITH YOURSELF

Tuva is a small country on the border of Mongolia and Siberia, a desolate place inhabited primarily by nomadic shepherds.

Some Tuvans have become fairly famous in the last decade because they can practice the art of *hömeï* (pronounced her-may), or throat singing. Tuvan throat singing, I can safely say, is like nothing I've ever heard before. Tuvan throat singers have mastered their vocal cords in such a way that they are able to sing two and even three notes at a time. It's a strange and beautiful sound, starting with a low bass note; then a higher melody is sung simultaneously. Thus a throat singer can harmonize with himself, a feat that is unique to Tuvans.

Meditatio calls for a similar feat, and one that also demands discipline and practice. Another way to think of making harmony with oneself during meditation is multitasking—doing two things at once, in this case with your mind instead of your throat.

The harmony called for in meditatio is to repeat the word or phrase over and over in your mind, almost like a mantra (*thrill . . . thrill . . . thrill*) while also paying attention to what feelings or emotions it provokes. As I chew on the word *thrill*, rolling it around in my mind, I'm also paying attention to how that word makes me feel. *Thrill* may make me experience excitement or fear or hope.

Here's another example. Let's say I've chosen the passage about Jesus' triumphal entry into Jerusalem on Palm Sunday for my lectio:

> *The people gave him a wonderful welcome, some throwing their coats on the street, others spreading out rushes they had cut in the fields. Running ahead and following after, they were calling out,*
>
> > *Hosanna!*
> > *Blessed is he who comes in God's name!*
> > *Blessed the coming kingdom of our father David!*
> > *Hosanna in highest heaven!*
>
> > *He entered Jerusalem, then entered the Temple. He looked around, taking it all in. But by now it was late, so he went back to Bethany with the Twelve.*
> > (Mark 11:8-11)

During my reading, the words that stick out are *he looked around*. As I spend time meditating on that phrase, the feeling that I notice in my gut is humiliation—even conviction. My meditation has brought these words of Scripture into contact with my soul, and what I sense is Jesus looking at me. I immediately want to know why. Why is Jesus looking at me? Why am I feeling this way? And when he looks at me, what does he see?

## DON'T MOVE ON . . . YET

One of the parts of lectio divina that I find most difficult has arrived—stopping for a while. My questions are for the next step, for oratio. The discipline of meditation is to stick with it for the full length of time allotted. To move too quickly into oratio (prayer) is to cheat yourself and to cheat God. God may have more to move into my heart than humiliation or conviction. Maybe, as I spend my time in meditation fully, my feeling of humiliation changes into a feeling of warmth and fulfillment.

God can do whatever he wants. As I read during the first step, he might take my mind from the word that initially stands out and bring another word to the forefront. Similarly, my imagination might settle on one particular emotion at first, but then God may bring something else to my mind and soul as the time goes by.

During meditation, as with every step of lectio divina, the most important advice I have for you is to slow down. It takes time to progress through the steps. Lectio divina can't be rushed. Actually, it can be, but it shouldn't be.

Slowing down is tough for me, and it will probably be tough for you. We live in a world that exemplifies the word *rush*. We're in a hurry to do almost everything. That makes lectio divina (and all types of contemplative prayer) countercultural for us. We live in a world of racecars; lectio divina is a horse and buggy. We communicate by instant messaging; lectio divina is communicating by smoke signals.

It will take a while for your body and soul to become familiar with this new pace. To slow down so much for twenty or thirty minutes a day will take discipline and practice, just as it takes discipline to stay in meditation for some minutes. Give it a try anyway—and don't give up, because the rewards are beyond our comprehension!

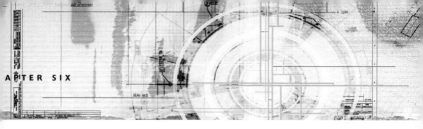

# CHAPTER SIX

# ORATIO

One of the first things that many of us learn when we're young is to pray. My two-year-old son, Tanner, insists that our whole family hold hands every time we sit down for a meal. Then he shouts proudly, "Dear Lord, give you peace. Amen!" Lily, who's eighteen months old, echoes loudly, "Amen!" Tanner's combination of prayer ("Dear Lord . . . ") and blessing ("May he give you peace") has become our grace before meals.

In bed at night, I'll ask Tanner if he wants to pray. His usual bedtime prayer is, "Dear Lord, I love Mommy and I love Daddy and I love Lily and I love . . . " Then he'll mention our dog, Beaumont, and proceed through all the relatives and friends he can think of.

Tanner can't read yet, though he has memorized a couple of Bible verses. He doesn't really understand the concept of God. He often asks, "Where is God?" Julie and I explain that, although God is in the room, we can't see him. We've only recently convinced him that our senior pastor isn't God!

But prayer he gets. He knows not only about the rhythms of prayer before meals and before bed, but also about the importance of speaking our hopes, wishes, and "loves" out to this unseen God.

Many of us have fond childhood memories of our parents kneeling at our bedsides, praying for us and with us. Or hearing the rhythms of the Lord's Prayer brings us back to a time when we were sitting next to our parents in church. I have specific memories of two friends praying for me during crucial times of grief (the death of a friend) and joy (graduation from high school).

Even when we haven't had memorable experiences in childhood, prayer is deep within our souls. It's our communication with the God who created us and loves us. Every human being who believes God exists longs to communicate with him. Far higher than the percentage of Americans who go to church weekly (48 percent) or read their Bibles weekly (39 percent) is the number of people who say they pray to God at least once a week (85 percent).[12] That's an overwhelmingly high percentage. We would be hard-pressed to find anything else other than eating, drinking, breathing, and sleeping that 85 percent of Americans do every week.

Whether it's a thirty-minute quiet time every morning or a few moments with him on the bus trip to school or a quick,

"Help, please!" before a test, God is on our minds a lot. We want to tell him what we're up to, what we're thinking about, our hopes and our fears—and we want to ask him for the things we need. As Christians, we believe God *is* standing nearby, ready to help, answer, comfort, and encourage us. He wants to give himself to us.

## GOD CAN HANDLE OUR TRUE FEELINGS

In the movie *The Apostle*, Robert Duvall plays Sonny, a preacher-evangelist who made a few mistakes in his life, one of them a *big* one. About one-third of the way into the movie, he's trying to figure out why these things have happened to him and why he showed such weakness in dealing with difficult circumstances. Estranged from his wife and children, he's staying in the attic at his mother's house, and he's making a lot of noise in the middle of the night. A neighbor calls to ask Sonny's mom what all the noise is about, and she responds, "Ever since he was a little boy, sometimes he talks to the Lord and sometimes he yells at him. Tonight he just happens to be yelling."

The image of Sonny pacing back and forth in his mother's attic, shouting at God—and in some ways shouting at himself—is a powerful image of prayer. It caught me off guard the first time I saw it, because it seemed so irreverent, so disrespectful of God. Most of us were brought up to think that

God demands our respect, and he does, but that doesn't mean we always need to be subdued.

Have you noticed how some people talk in normal voices until the moment they begin to pray? Then they'll suddenly lower their voices to a whisper. This is, I suppose, a way to show reverence and respect, the way you might talk to a king or a president whom you fear. Although this may be an appropriate way to approach God at times, it seems like this is the way you approach a father who's waiting to give you a smack with a wooden spoon, not a father who's going to hug you, wrap you in the finest cloak, and throw you a banquet.

This is why I appreciate Sonny's prayer in the attic. He's got nothing to hide from God, because God already knows his every thought. He's frustrated with God, upset by the way things are going in his life, and he's not going to hide that fact. He wants to work these things out with God, and he's honest enough to let God have it, to get in God's face. He knows God can handle it.

We find a biblical example of a heated exchange between God and a man in Exodus 32. It's pure speculation to guess how it all went down between Moses and God on Mount Sinai, but the tone of the recorded conversation between the two is not exactly calm. "Stop your anger," Moses says to God,

"Think twice" (verse 12). Ultimately, God changes his mind as a result of Moses' urgent pleadings.

## FAITHFUL URGENCY

Oratio, the third step of lectio divina, can have the same kind of urgency Sonny and Moses display before God. Having read the selected passage and meditated to the point of awareness of some emotion or feeling, it's time to work out with God exactly what that means.

First and foremost, oratio is a conversation: "God, why did you give me this word today? Why did I feel this when I meditated on it?" In classical Latin, *oratio* means speaking, speech, or language, especially eloquent speech like an imperial address. Centuries later, in church Latin, it came to mean prayer or speech directed at God.

The word *orant* is a related term that signifies a figure found in many early Christian paintings, for instance, in the catacombs of Rome. An orant is a person standing with arms raised in prayer. Arms raised and hands open is a posture of receiving and openness, not only asking God a question, but also being ready to hear his answer.

Let's think about Psalm 1 again. Remember that in my reading, the word *thrill* stood out for me. Now's the time for me to ask, "God, why did you want me to rest with the word *thrill*? And why did I feel excitement as I meditated on that word?" There's a lot of implicit faith in questions like these. Just as easily I could have picked *thrill* for my own selfish reasons. Maybe I didn't allow God to be part of the process and went ahead on my own.

To counter these doubts, think about these two points: Questioning whether God gave you the word is a waste of time, because it's nearly impossible to know. Sorting out what's attributable to you and what's attributable to God during the process of lectio divina is like separating noodles from spaghetti sauce once they've been mixed together. Even if you could do it, it's just too messy. Second, God can use our self-ishly motivated choices if he wants to, so it doesn't matter what's from him and what's from you. Even if you chose the word and didn't give God a voice in the process, he's still God, and he can still use it. Ultimately, it's still his Word!

Why do I feel excitement as I meditate on the word *thrill*? Now I'll converse with God about this very question. How am I excited by God's plan in my life right now? What do I find thrilling about meditating on his Word? What does that mean for me in the future? What will I take away from my lectio divina today that will guide me? These are questions I wrestle with during oratio.

The other example I gave in the last chapter was the Palm Sunday passage. I was drawn to the phrase "he looked around," and I felt humiliation and embarrassment as I meditated on Jesus looking around in my life. As I admitted in the last chapter, I'm often tempted to jump right through meditatio and into oratio too quickly. Once I've gotten in touch with my feelings, I immediately want to talk to God so I can figure them out. So here I have to preach patience to myself once again, spending enough time in meditatio to let the words and feelings sink into my soul.

When the time does come to move into oratio, I go right to God. I know as I'm going into this prayer that God doesn't like me to feel humiliated. Being a God of grace, he doesn't humiliate people into doing as he pleases. I know that the humiliation I feel is about me and my struggle. I also become aware quickly that my feelings of embarrassment are about a certain sin in my life.

My prayer of questioning moves into a prayer of asking for forgiveness and healing. The time of oratio should be about moving through the entire experience with God and working toward resolution on some level. The ultimate question in oratio is this: Lord, what do you want me to do with what you've given me today? In lectio divina, we're working under the faithful assumption that God has brought the word and the feeling to the surface, and our question is always "Why?"

Oratio could be called the life-application portion of lectio divina, although I use that term cautiously. One of the dangers in modern Bible reading is always reading the text with the goal of making a personal application. For some passages application makes perfect sense, but for others, it's a stretch. For instance, you can probably find something to apply to your life in Romans or Galatians, but it's more difficult with things such as lists of ceremonial law from Deuteronomy or prophetic passages of Revelation.

Youth pastors share an inside joke about what-it-means-to-me Bible studies. Those are the small-group sessions during which members share what the passages under discussion mean to them. Often the individual interpretations are so far off from each other that no consensus of interpretation could ever be developed.

The difference in lectio divina is that we're trying to hear personal words from God. We're not trying to arrive at a group consensus. A group setting is one of the best ways to practice lectio divina, but the goal is not for everyone to hear the same word. In fact, if that ever happens, be sure to give even more credit to the Holy Spirit!

So listen for God's response after you ask him why. Be attuned to what he has to say to you. And then try to work with him on what that means for your life. What do you take away?

## THE INNER DIALOGUE

The ideas and specific questions I've given you are somewhat artificial, meant to spur you on in your prayer and to give you some idea where to start with oratio. As you become more experienced, you'll find less and less need to ask God these straightforward questions. Instead, you'll probably ease into a natural conversation, just as you do when you talk to your best friend.

Here are two pieces of advice about oratio by Bernardo Olivera, the Abbot General of the Cistercian monks, maybe the people most familiar with lectio divina:

> *Having listened by reading and meditation, you can now speak in prayer. If you know what the text says and what the text says to you, what do you say to him?*
>
> *Silence can also be a response, as much for the one who prays, carried out of himself, as for him who knows all.*[13]

You see the dilemma: Should I talk or should I be silent and listen? Father Olivera suggests both are appropriate at different times. When you talk to your best friend, you probably flow between talking and listening quite naturally. You don't even think much about the process. It just happens.

We may find it harder to perfect the flow of conversation with God, particularly because we can't see him sitting in front of us, nor do we hear him in an audible way. Eastern Orthodox Christianity, which is practiced in Russia, Greece, and Eastern Europe among other areas, emphasizes the biblical truth that God through his Holy Spirit resides within us more than other streams of Christianity. Here in the West, we more often emphasize God as sovereign, transcendent, and outside of us. Both, of course, are true and biblical. But our Orthodox brothers and sisters remind us that we can become quiet and look within to hear the Lord, as well as look outside of ourselves to hear from God.

As we become more experienced, the rhythms of inner dialogue between God and us take over. Thelma Hall writes, "Eventually a gradual simplification begins to take place."[14] Prayer becomes simpler over time, and the conversation between you and God will become more and more natural. As you progress in lectio divina, you will find books like this less helpful, because you'll discover your own patterns and rhythms of prayer.

Be gentle with yourself during oratio. Give prayer enough time to develop. Be patient and listen for God, tell God about what's on your heart, and pay attention to the movements of prayer that work best for you.

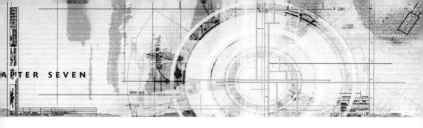

# CONTEMPLATIO

Writing about contemplation is strange. It's weird because the fourth step of lectio divina is so unlike our everyday activities. The first three steps of lectio divina aren't that difficult to describe, because we read, think, and pray every day. Those are activities we're accustomed to. Contemplatio, on the other hand, is an inactivity.

The move from oratio to contemplatio is mostly an act of letting go. Contemplation is inner quietness. The transition from the active prayer of oratio to the silence of contemplatio is gradual and gentle.

In Latin, *contemplatio* means considering a concept with the heart or the mind. While that may seem to be an activity, *considering* stands in contrast to *doing*. Some ancient philosophers thought that the best life possible would be a purely contemplative one, and this concept of the ideal life has persisted even into our own time. Maybe you've heard about some of the computer scientists who believe that one day human beings will be able to shed our bodies, download all the information we need into a computer-brain, and live in utter contemplation. This idea directly contradicts the Christian understanding of life, in which body and spirit are inextricably united.

For Christians, contemplation is a discipline in which we don't give up our bodies, but we temporarily quiet our bodies and minds for one purpose: to rest in God's love. An anonymous Christian mystic who lived in England in the fourteenth century wrote a book called *The Cloud of Unknowing*, which is considered one of the best books ever written on contemplation. Here are some instructions from that book:

> *Here is what you are to do: lift your heart up to the Lord, with a gentle stirring of love desiring him for his own sake and not for his gifts. Center all your attention and desire on him and let this be the sole concern of your mind and heart. Do all in your power to forget everything else, keeping your thoughts and desires free from involvement with any of God's creatures or their affairs in general or in particular. Perhaps this will seem like an irresponsible attitude, but I tell you, let them all be; pay no attention to them.*[15]

This final step of lectio divina, the utter rest and comfort and silence that come as we rest in the arms of our loving Savior, is a wonderful gift, no matter how disturbing or shocking the word you received that day may have been.

## GOD WHISPERS TO ELIJAH AND MARY

Two instances come to mind of people who found God in quiet moments. After God humiliated the prophets of Baal with one of the best bonfires of all time, God's prophet Elijah had to flee from Israel because Queen Jezebel and her army were out to get him. He fled for forty days, making it all the way to Mount Horeb, where he took up residence in a cave. The word of God told Elijah to stand at attention at the top of the mountain and wait for God to pass by. He did, and this is what happened:

> *A hurricane ripped through the mountains and shat-*
> *tered the rocks before God, but God wasn't to be found*
> *in the wind; after the wind an earthquake, but God*
> *wasn't in the earthquake; and after the earthquake*
> *fire, but God wasn't in the fire; and after the fire a*
> *gentle and quiet whisper.* (1 Kings 19:11-12)

In a quiet whisper, God spoke his plans for Israel to Elijah. We can only imagine how nervous Elijah must have been at the top of the mountain, waiting for God to speak out of the vehement and dangerous elements of a hurricane, earthquake, and fire, bracing himself for an experience with the Lord that might kill him. Instead, God waited for those thunderous moments to pass, and in the deafening quiet that followed, God whispered to Elijah.

We often think of the God of the universe speaking in majesty with thunder and lightning. We think of a God so explosive and powerful that even hearing his voice would be overwhelming to a human being. But here's a case of God speaking in the quietest voice imaginable. As usual, God does not conform to our expectations.

In the tenth chapter of Luke's gospel, we find another story of someone finding God in quietness and stillness. It's the story of two sisters and Jesus' visit to their home:

> *As they continued their travel, Jesus entered a village. A woman by the name of Martha welcomed him and made him feel quite at home. She had a sister, Mary, who sat before the Master, hanging on every word he said. But Martha was pulled away by all she had to do in the kitchen. Later, she stepped in, interrupting them. "Master, don't you care that my sister has abandoned the kitchen to me? Tell her to lend me a hand."*
>
> *The Master said, "Martha, dear Martha, you're fussing far too much and getting yourself*

*worked up over nothing. One thing only is essential,
and Mary has chosen it—it's the main course, and
it won't be taken from her."* (Luke 10:38-42)

The author of *The Cloud of Unknowing* wrote of this passage,
"Mary turned to Jesus with all the love of her heart. . . . She sat
there in perfect stillness with her heart's secret, joyous love intent
upon that cloud of unknowing between her and her God."[16] Mary
didn't pester Jesus with questions; she didn't fuss about what she
could get for him; she didn't tell him all the things she needed.
Mary sat at Jesus' feet and absorbed every word he said, and she
absorbed his presence. She reveled in his love.

Jesus makes an interesting point to Martha when she com-
plains about getting stuck with all the kitchen work. He says
that what Mary has received during this time at his feet "won't
be taken from her." We can't really blame Martha, because she
didn't know that Jesus' time on earth would be so short, but
when it was all said and done, probably no one remembered
what a good meal Martha prepared that day. Mary, on the
other hand, always had those moments with the Lord, and she
must have treasured them the rest of her life.

Like Martha, we're so often tempted to fill our lives, even
our spiritual and prayer lives, with activity. We live in a fast-
paced society. The practice of our Christian faith often mirrors

the busyness in the rest of our lives. The small group of high school seniors meeting at my house on Mondays often has this urgency. Someone comes late, rushing in right after a soccer match, and two others have to leave early because they've got a big project due on Tuesday morning. This is not an indictment of these seniors. They're simply living the way they know, the way that has been modeled for them by their parents and peers.

The key to another way to approach the Christian life is contemplatio. It's to be more Mary-like, to know the importance of stopping all activity — ceasing activity of the body and the mind — and sitting at the feet of Jesus. Listening in the silence to his every word, and, even more importantly, simply feeling, noticing, and absorbing how much he loves you.

We know less about other examples of quiet communion in the Bible, but we can guess some of these biblical figures may have had contemplatio-like times with the Lord: Moses during his forty-day sojourn on Mount Sinai; Jesus during those times he withdrew from the crowds to pray in a quiet place; Paul while he sat in prison; John when he was in exile on the island of Patmos. We have these examples and more of people in the Bible and in the history of the church who have spent significant time in silence with God. Remember, none of these individuals had a study Bible on his lap or a CD player with Christian music filling her ears. Instead, each was completely alone—in the quiet with God.

## HURDLES

"My mind wanders."

"I keep hearing the song that I just listened to in my car."

"I don't even realize that I'm thinking about what I've got to do tomorrow, and then I'm totally distracted. It's so frustrating!"

I not only hear these exasperated cries from students, but I also experience them myself. The utter quiet that we long for in contemplatio is easier said than done. To find external quiet can be hard enough. Depending on your home, you may have to wake up half an hour before everyone else to find silence. Or maybe you'll have to go to the library during your study hour or out to a park after school to find some quiet.

Internal quiet is another thing altogether. Sometimes it seems as if the quieter my surroundings are, the louder my internal distractions become. How do you quiet your mind and rest in the presence and love of God?

The first piece of advice I have is this: Don't beat yourself up for getting distracted. Contemplatio is difficult, requiring significant practice and discipline. I don't say this to scare you from trying it or to lower your expectations. All you can do is your best. Get as quiet as you can get. If something distracts you, gently and quietly move back into silence and put the distraction aside, because ultimately, the fruit of contemplatio is a gift of the Holy Spirit. Like so many other aspects of spiritual life, you can't earn or achieve inner peace with God. The experience is different for everyone, and the results are always an unmerited gift from God's Spirit.

Let's go back to *The Cloud of Unknowing* once more, where the author writes about how contemplatio is different for everyone:

> *The truth is that God, in his wisdom, determines the course and the character of each one's contemplative journey according to the talents and gifts he has given. It is true that some people do not reach contemplation without long and arduous spiritual toil and even then only now and again know its perfection in the delight of ecstasy called ravishing. Yet, there are others so spiritually refined by grace and so intimate with God in prayer that they seem to possess and experience the perfection of this work almost as they like, even in the midst of their ordinary daily routine, whether sitting, standing, walking, or kneeling.*

*They manage to retain full control and use of their*
*physical and spiritual faculties at all times.*[17]


So don't give up. Gracefully accept whatever God gives in your contemplation. God loves you as only the One who created you can. His love is unconditional and unending. Sit at his feet; absorb his presence; allow him to hold you. That's what contemplatio is all about.


## COMING UP FOR AIR

Leaving contemplatio is a lot like resurfacing after swimming underwater. When your time of contemplatio is over, let your mind and spirit move gently and slowly out of lectio divina. I've found a good conclusion for lectio divina is the Lord's Prayer—familiar, comforting, and a reminder of God's presence in my life one more time as I conclude.

As you spend more time praying lectio divina, you'll probably find that you don't want to jump up and get going to your next appointment. You'll want to sit for a few moments and allow your mind to consciously process what you have experienced. If you've ever received a professional massage, the experience is something like that. You feel totally relaxed but highly alert and completely fulfilled.

Reentering your normal world can be a little depressing, too, especially if you've had a particularly excellent time with God. Facilitate your reentry by using a *florilegium* (floor-i-LEG-i-um), a notebook used by monks to record the passages they've used for lectio divina and what God said to them through those passages. In Latin, it means "picking flowers"—seeing the beauty in what God says through his Word.

Another benefit of keeping a florilegium is to see how God says different things through the same passage depending on our states of mind or places in life. You might use the same psalm for lectio divina that you used a year ago and hear a completely different word from God. This is not a sign of weakness, but a mark that lectio divina works! As the psalmist sings, "The revelation of God is whole and pulls our lives together" (19:7). God's Word is alive—it always has new ideas, new meanings, and new ways it can inspire us to live a Christian life.

# PART THREE

# EXPERIENCING LECTIO DIVINA

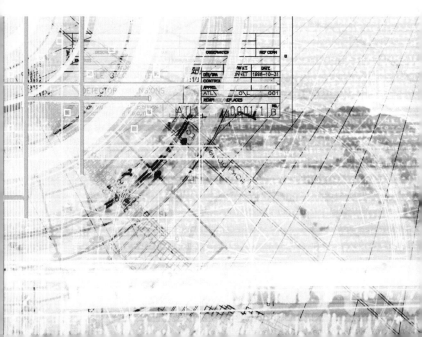

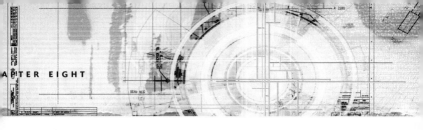

# CHAPTER EIGHT

# A PERSONAL LECTIO DIVINA
## WITH ME

It's early June in Minnesota—my favorite time of the year—as I write this. In youth ministry, we're in that breathing space between school-year programming and summer trips and camps, so I've taken a week of study leave to read, write, and pray. I'm up at our family's cabin, on a lake in the woods of north-central Minnesota. Sitting on 160 acres, the cabin is secluded. I'm here alone for a few days—until my wife and kids join me.

Actually, I'm not completely alone. Beaumont, my yellow Labrador, is here with me. He's the perfect companion. He likes to go on walks and boat rides, but he never turns on the stereo or starts talking while I'm writing or praying.

I like to get up early when I'm here, so the alarm goes off at 5:30, when it's already light outside. I pull on some clothes and swing through the kitchen to start the coffeemaker. Then I go out the back door where Beaumont's waiting. Although Beaumont's happy to see me, he's especially happy because I feed him first thing in the morning. I open the garage door and pour him a bowl of food. After he eats, we begin our daily walk down the road.

From the county road, we access our cabin by a mile-long stretch that's not much more than two tire ruts. It wends through huge white pines and a patch of new-growth aspen and curves alongside a slough of cattails and lily pads. On the walk, a variety of birds greet Beaumont and me. Fresh deer tracks on the road are evidence that we scared one off.

Back at the cabin, I pour a cup of coffee, grab my Bible, and head down the path to the lake. We have a dock with a bench on it facing west, a favorite place to watch sunsets. The day is already warm, so I throw a stick into the lake, and Beaumont happily jumps in. Having retrieved it, he takes up residence at my feet and begins to whittle the large stick into myriad toothpicks with his teeth.

## READING THE PASSAGE

This morning, I've allowed the lectionary to choose my text. Actually, the lectionary assigns four passages per day, so I've got some choice in the matter. I've picked the one that's most obscure to me, one from the prophet Hosea. I know almost nothing about him. I must have dozed off during that class in seminary.

I think the whole passage in the lectionary is too long, so I decide to use only the first part, Hosea 6:1-3.

> Come on, let's go back to GOD.
>> He hurt us, but he'll heal us.
> He hit us hard,
>> but he'll put us right again.
> In a couple of days we'll feel better.
>> By the third day he'll have made us brand-new,
> Alive and on our feet,
>> fit to face him.
> We're ready to study GOD,
>> eager for God-knowledge.
> As sure as dawn breaks,
>> so sure is his daily arrival.
> He comes as rain comes,
>> as spring rain refreshes the ground.

I read the passage over and over. Just when I think I've read it enough times, I read it again. I even have the chance to read it out loud—loudly—because no one is on the lake this morning. Finally, I stop reading after twenty-five or thirty times through the verses.

At first, I keep getting hung up on the words *third day*. I think about the band by that name. I wonder if they took their name from this verse or just from the fact that Jesus rose on the third day. This is one of the reasons I keep reading the passage over and over again, because I want to get beyond this distraction to listen for the word God has for me.

What I hear as I continue is *brand new*. I love *The Message* because the language is fresh. I find this phrase, *brand new*, refreshing.

## MULLING IT OVER

Having finished my reading, I put the Bible down on the bench beside me and gently slide into meditatio. I think about things that are brand new: a newborn baby, a spring tulip, a new CD, a new book that's never been opened.

The sun is coming up behind me. I open my eyes and think about today being a brand-new day, full of opportunities and choices. What a great day it will be—warm and sunny. Honestly, I can hardly think of a place I'd rather be or a day I'd rather be starting.

Before heading too far down that road and moving into oratio too soon, I decide to close my eyes and mull over the phrase some more. *Brand new.* I form the words with my mind's eye. Like the screen saver where the time bounces and flips around the screen, I see the phrase *brand new* bouncing around in my head, back and forth, up and down, flipping around.

Meanwhile, I can hear birds singing and the occasional fish jumping in the lake. I take a long loon call as a good indicator of time to move into oratio.

My mind is predisposed to think about things theologically, so I immediately begin to think about the brand-new beginning that we each have with Jesus Christ. In many ways, his crucifixion and resurrection was the start of history; everything before those two events was prehistory.

I think about the apostle Paul asserting that in Christ the old has passed away; everything has become new.

I think about the New Testament being a brand-new way of having a covenant between God and humankind.

I drift into a prayer of thanksgiving. How awesome to follow and worship a God who allows second chances and who makes everything brand new.

## LOOKING INWARD

Then I start to look inward, toward the places in my life where I need to be made brand new. I find plenty. I ask God to give me a brand-new heart of love for my family, for my job, for myself.

I think about my job. It's June. I'm facing a long summer — two mission trips and two weeks at camp. Four weeks away from my family. While I haven't admitted it out loud, I know the thought of leaving them for four weeks during the summer is taking a toll on me. How I look at youth ministry has changed now that I have two children. I realize it's time for me to deal with God on this issue.

*What does this mean, God?* The big issue is whether I can stay at the job I presently have. The more immediate issue, the one tied to *brand new,* is that I need to be given a brand-new heart and spirit for the upcoming summer. I know I need these, and I need them now, so I go into overdrive prayer to ask God for both.

After several minutes of productive and encouraging prayer on this subject, I begin to let go of all the anxiety I'm feeling about the summer. I know it's time to move toward contemplatio.

As usual, during contemplatio I focus on my breathing, slowing it down, evening it out. The air here in the north woods is so clean that I enjoy breathing deeply. As I breathe, I allow myself to sink into God's love—to plunge in, as the monk Thomas Merton wrote.

## ON WITH THE DAY

I don't know how long I've been in contemplatio, but I'm brought out of it rudely. Beaumont is shaking water all over me! Today it's fine. I've experienced a wonderful prayer time; I couldn't be happier with where God has taken me. What an awesome journey this life with God is!

I feel the appropriate response is to shout my belief to the world, so I stand up, walk to the end of the dock, and loudly state for all the world—at least the lake, birds, fish, and ducks—to hear:

> *I believe in God, the Father almighty,*
> *    creator of heaven and earth.*
>
> *I believe in Jesus Christ, his only Son, our Lord.*
> *He was conceived by the power of the Holy Spirit*
> *    and born of the Virgin Mary.*
> *He suffered under Pontius Pilate,*
> *    was crucified, died, and was buried.*

*He descended to the dead.*
*On the third day he rose again.*
*He ascended into heaven,*
     *and is seated at the right hand of the Father.*
*He will come again to judge the living and the dead.*


*I believe in the Holy Spirit,*
     *the holy catholic church,*
     *the communion of saints,*
     *the forgiveness of sins,*
     *the resurrection of the body,*
     *and the life everlasting.*


*Amen.*[18]


I can't imagine a better benediction for my prayer time than the Apostles' Creed.

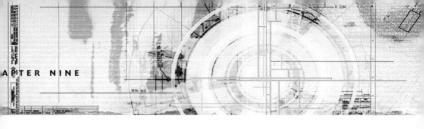

# CHAPTER NINE

## LECTIO DIVINA
### WITH MY SMALL GROUP

A small group of high school seniors meets at our house on Monday evenings. Every week, they gather with Julie and me on our couches in the basement, munching popcorn and sipping Diet Cokes.

At the time of this small-group lectio divina, it's mid-February, so we spend at least half an hour every time we're together this semester talking about next year. Charlie's waiting to hear from Seattle Pacific University. Erin has to choose between Seattle Pacific and Westmont College. Chad has been accepted at a couple of schools, but he's waiting to hear from a few more. Just this week, Carrie was offered a full-ride soccer scholarship by San Diego State University. Brenna's headed for the University of St. Thomas in Minnesota. Katy is working on her application to spend a year with Youth With A Mission. Heidi's waiting to hear back from the University of Hawaii. (We're all extremely jealous: She gets to go on a campus visit.)

We've also spent the year trying to get our arms around the entire Bible, reading a chapter each week from Walt Wangerin's novelized version, *The Book of God*. But deep in the heart of a Minnesota winter, our group has fallen into a rut. Everyone still comes every week, but most aren't reading the chapter consistently. We've been reading from the Old Testament for almost six months. Although we're just about to make the turn into the New Testament, I figure a one-week diversion will help.

On many nights, we have a fire in the fireplace, lots of food in the basement, and the dog knocking over soda cans with his tail. Instead of all that activity, Julie and I tried to make the area more peaceful. I cleaned up all the toys, and we placed a three-wick candle — to represent the Trinity — on the coffee table.

After our college updates and a brief report on Jeremiah from Katy (the only person who read the chapter), it's almost nine o'clock when we're ready to start lectio divina. I can tell that a couple of kids who still have homework to finish are getting antsy. I remind them that they're second-semester seniors, so they don't have too much to worry about. I've used up most of my patience reserves to get everyone settled enough to pray.

## THE PREPARATION

All the members of our small group have done lectio divina before, so they know the drill. I start by reminding them about contemplative prayer by saying something like this: "We've all got a lot on our minds tonight, me included. Chad's got a math quiz tomorrow, Julie's got a busy day with the kids, Charlie's got his internship, and I've got meetings from 7:30 A.M. until 9:00 P.M. All of our activities will try to creep into our lectio divina. When this happens, don't get upset with yourself. Just gently repel the distractions with your word. This is all about us getting quiet and listening for God. Ultimately, it's about resting in God's love."

A couple of the kids have their eyes closed as I'm saying these things. Some are shifting on their couches, getting comfortable. Others find their cell phones and turn them off. Brenna pulls the comforter up to her neck; Heidi puts down the kid's toy she is fiddling with. I have the sense that they all need this experience.

I know it may sound strange, but I'm a little fearful of doing lectio divina with my small group. You see, we've had an awesome year together, and we've gotten close as we've read through the whole Old Testament. We've had to tackle some tough issues, and we've been quite honest with each other about our lives.

I'm afraid I'll get this reaction: *There goes Tony imposing another of his spiritual disciplines on us again.* While it may not seem strange for a youth pastor to steer the group one way or another, that's not the kind of relationship I have with this group of students. I'm one of the members, an equal part. We decided together what to read this year and what time to meet. We meet at our house only so Julie and I don't have to hire a babysitter every week (not to mention that both of our babysitters are in the group!).

So I made the decision to lead the group through lectio divina with some trepidation and much humility. Of course, I should have been assured that the experience would be great—and it was! God moved gently and quietly in our group, and I should never have doubted that he would.

## THE STORY OF THE LOST SHEEP

Most of us are familiar with parables, probably because they're generally easy for Sunday school teachers to explain using a flannel graph. Parables are, however, much more significant than just telling us to be nice to our neighbors. They're Jesus' way of describing the kingdom of God.

The fifteenth chapter of Luke is taken up with a trio of stories that explains what happens in the kingdom of God when someone is lost—what God does when one of his creations wanders away and can't find him.

I explain this broader context to the group; then I read the first parable, the Story of the Lost Sheep.

> *By this time a lot of men and women of doubtful reputation were hanging around Jesus, listening intently. The Pharisees and religion scholars were not pleased, not at all pleased. They growled, "He takes in sinners and eats meals with them, treating them like old friends." Their grumbling triggered this story.*
>
> *"Suppose one of you had a hundred sheep and lost one. Wouldn't you leave the ninety-nine in the wilderness and go after the lost one until you found it? When found, you can be sure you would put it across your shoulders, rejoicing, and when you got home call in your friends and neighbors, saying, 'Celebrate with me! I've found my lost sheep!' Count on it—there's more joy in heaven over one sinner's rescued life than over ninety-nine good people in no need of rescue."* (verses 1-7)

I announce that we will have a few minutes of silence before I start reading again. (I like to have different people read, but I decide that on this occasion I will read the passage every time. I'm aware that not everyone in our group likes to read out loud. I'm also springing the whole lectio divina process on them as a group anyway, so I don't want to spring reading out loud on them, too. Some people get so anxious about reading out loud that they have a hard time concentrating on prayer.)

After a short silence, I say, "Now I'll read our passage again. Listen for the word or phrase that stands out for you. What word is God giving you?"

Three times I read,

> " 'Celebrate with me! I've found my lost sheep!' Count on it—there's more joy in heaven over one sinner's rescued life than over ninety-nine good people in no need of rescue."

## CONTINUING IN MEDITATION, PRAYER, AND CONTEMPLATION

We sit in silence for a couple of minutes. Then I ask people to say the word or phrase that God has given them:

> Good people
> Rescued life
> Celebrate with me

> *Lost sheep*
> *Found*
> *Celebrate with me*
> *Celebrate with me*
> *Joy in heaven*
> *Count on it (my answer)*

I explain the next step, meditatio, as chewing on that word. "Don't move forward yet," I explain. "Just chew on the word with your mind and pay attention to how you feel as a result." Then I read the passage two more times.

After some silence, I invite people to share what they are experiencing. Not everyone shares out loud, but here are some of the responses:

> *Rescued life* and newness or new beginning
> *Celebrate with me* — joy, happiness, party
> *Lost sheep* and sadness
> *Celebrate with me* and relief
> *Joy in heaven* — party

As I meditate on *count on it*, I feel a solidity, firmness, confidence, surety. Actually, I see an image of an Egyptian pyramid with a strong foundation that cannot be moved.

I explain that the time has come to talk with God in prayer about what it means—this word and this emotion—and to listen for his response. I read the passage again.

In the minutes that follow, I sense from God that Jesus' words *Count on it* are a challenge to me to have faith in what he says. God seems to be saying, "Listen! These words of Jesus are sure things. You can count on those words, and you can count on the one who said them." I find the time of prayer to be comforting and even joyful as I bask in the solidness and reliability of Jesus' words.

We don't share our prayers out loud, but after a few more minutes, I encourage everyone to set all words, images, and feelings aside to spend the last minutes in contemplation, simply resting in God's loving arms.

Finally, I close the lectio divina time with a brief prayer:

> *Lord God, thank you for your Word, which is inspired and inspiring. You've spoken to each of us tonight, given each one of us a message through your Word. May we carry it with us as we move into the week and often be brought back to the feeling of resting in your loving arms. In Jesus' name, Amen.*

## WHAT THE SENIORS THINK

We don't take the time to go around the group and share because time is short and I want to respect their privacy. But as the seniors are putting on their coats to leave, I let them know they can e-mail me about their experiences this evening.

Here are the e-mails I receive:

> Tonight was really interesting for me. I really like what we did and I felt this was a new beginning for me. I felt that God was talking to me and telling me that I have found what is not good in my life and turned it around. I feel like he was telling me that I am a strong person and I can do anything I want to do. I think that is why the word "found" stuck out for me so much. I felt like God was saying that I have found what I was missing in my life and what I need to do is follow my heart. He also told me that if I follow my dreams my future will be very good, and I will be very happy. I have no idea why all of this came about, but I think that is the cool thing about it — it's like the Lord works in mysterious ways. I don't know — I just thought this whole thing was kind of eye opening and I left feeling relieved and

refreshed, like I'm ready for anything that comes at me. It's kind of weird to think that God was talking to me and telling me that. The whole experience was good.


hey Tony — tonight I really liked the prayer idea I think it was a good change up because I think our group was in a little rut. The phrase that stuck out for me was "celebrate with me" and I'm not quite sure why. I don't know if that meant that I have a strong faith and I should bring others into it with me and give them all of the opportunities that I have, even if I won't know how they will react. Or maybe just saying to enjoy my life right now, because after seeing a bunch of friends from another church retreat this past weekend and talking with them, I realized what a good situation I am in — with my faith, my friends, and my lifestyle. I think God was just telling me to be happy and make the effort to let others know about all of the awesome opportunities they could have — and just have a positive outlook on everything. I dunno, that's what I got out of it, and it was a good thing to do ... we should do that every once in a while I think.

I just wanted to tell you what I thought of the prayer that we did (I really have no clue how to spell it). I really, really like it, but it frustrates me so badly—I mean here I am trying my darndest to sit and be at one with God and truly be quiet, and I find my mind wandering to subjects such as dresses for the Sweetheart Dance. That's right, I couldn't be quiet with God 'cause I was preoccupied with dresses. What a joke. Before that when we were picking the words that stood out to us, upon the first reading I liked the "celebrate with me," but later when I was repeating it in my head all that I heard was that hip '70s song "celebrate good times...come on!" So I decided that that set of words was more distracting than helpful to my spiritual experience. I think we should do that more often though. I know it would be helpful for me to practice being quiet with myself and with God. So there you have it, I loved it and was frustrated for most of the time.

hey Tony, last night's small group was cool. Lexio devina (don't know how to spell it...) is one of my favorite prayers you do with us. Despite the difficulty of keeping your mind from wandering, it's amazing to see what word or phrase God is going to show you. Every time I have done it God says something new. No matter where I am in the business of my own life, God takes whatever verse is being read and forms it to spark something within me. Last night the phrase I heard was "Celebrate with me." Through the meditation and reflection processes I realized that God was telling me I am very excited about him. That whatever comes of my plans for after high school, I need to celebrate his life, and that comforted me. He made me feel like it will work out because I realize what is important.

All of my concerns about springing this method of prayer on the seniors without them wanting it are allayed. Their responses confirm that lectio divina is a powerful and profound tool for a small group.

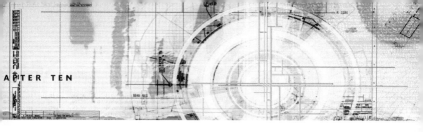

# CHAPTER TEN

# LECTIO DIVINA
## WITH MY YOUTH GROUP

It's 7:30 on a Sunday night in August, so it's just getting dusky. Our church's youth room is fairly large, with high ceilings. It lends itself to contemplative prayer quite well. But, to avoid distractions, I've covered the pool table and pushed the foosball table and pinball machine against the wall.

I want students and adults who enter the room to think that in some way they've left their daily experience and entered into a transcendent, holy space. I want the room to have an otherworldly feel. The lights are dim and I've placed candles all around the room. Candles have a unique ability to bring a room to life without overwhelming it with light. The couches are pushed into groups that seat eight to ten people each. Participants walk through a cloud of fragrant smoke as they enter the room. (About a year ago I purchased a censer—an incense burner—and incense and charcoal from an Eastern Orthodox supplier.)

I've got ancient Christian music playing on the sound system. Tonight I've chosen a CD called *Byzantine Chant*.[19] It's otherworldly and adds to the atmosphere. The projector is on; PowerPoint slowly scrolls through images of Jesus on the big screen. This heightens the holy sense of the space and gives people a focal point for their reflection as they wait for the prayer to begin. People instinctively leave their shoes in the hall.

## WELCOME TO THE DEEPENING

We call this night The Deepening. We hold it once each month to explore ancient contemplative prayer exercises. Although the youth ministry sponsors the evening, plenty of adults show up. Many students and adults come with their small groups, and they sit together. Others come alone and sit wherever they wish.

When we have a critical mass gathered, I welcome people and give announcements. I don't want to interrupt once we get going, and I don't want my announcements to be the last thing they hear. I want people to leave with a word from God in their minds.

I ask people to introduce themselves to the others in their circles. While some circles know each other well from their small group meetings, many people have never met. It's important that they at least know each others' names before they share what can be an intimate, vulnerable experience.

Then I grab the guitar and play a few mellow worship songs. This isn't the time for anything new or difficult. We sing familiar, repetitive tunes. Enough about the evening will be unfamiliar, so well-known songs give a sense of security.

Next I explain the history of lectio divina—not an involved lecture, but a brief outline of the practice to give the people context for their prayers. (I realize not everyone is as enamored with history as I am, but I like to know the background of a spiritual discipline before I try it.) The purpose of The Deepening is simply to introduce ancient spiritual practices. Individuals can decide for themselves which practices they'd like to make a part of their daily spiritual disciplines. We're all putting more tools in our toolboxes, but, just as with a handyman's tools, we'll use some more than others.

As I explain lectio divina, I project two quotations onto the screen:

> *One day I was engaged in physical work with my hands and I began to think about the spiritual tasks we humans have. While I was thinking, four spiritual steps came to mind: reading (lectio), meditation (meditatio), prayer (oratio), and contemplation (contemplatio). This is the ladder of monastics by*

*which they are lifted up from the earth into heaven.
There are only a few distinct steps, but the distance
covered is beyond measure and belief since the lower
part is fixed on the earth and its top passes through
the clouds to lay bare the secrets of heaven.*[20]

—GUIGO II

*It is not a method, but rather a type of free-form,
serious play.*[21]                                    —KATHLEEN NORRIS

## REFLECTING ON PSALM 67

I think that choosing a passage for a group lectio divina is
frightening. By that I mean it's tempting to choose a passage I
think my kids need to hear when that's for God to determine,
not me. Less dangerous but just as tempting is the desire to
pick a passage that means a lot to me. While that text may be
meaningful to others as well, I don't want to impose my spiritual experiences on others.

Consequently, when I lead lectio divina with groups, I most
often turn to a passage in the lectionary. (If you need a reminder
about lectionaries, see Picking the Passage, in chapter 4.) Old
Testament lessons are assigned from Genesis and Isaiah, an
epistle lesson from Romans, and a gospel lesson from Matthew.
For this Sunday, the lectionary gives two choices from the

Psalter: Psalms 67 and 133. When I introduce the lectio divina practice to people for the first time, I want to use a passage that lends itself to reflection. I settle on Psalm 67:

> God, mark us with grace
> and blessing! Smile!
> The whole country will see how you work,
> all the godless nations see how you save.
> God! Let people thank and enjoy you.
> Let all people thank and enjoy you.
> Let all far-flung people become happy
> and shout their happiness because
> You judge them fair and square,
> you tend the far-flung peoples.
> God! Let all people thank and enjoy you.
> Let all people thank and enjoy you.
> Earth, display your exuberance!
> You mark us with blessing, O God, our God.
> You mark us with blessing, O God.
> Earth's four corners — honor him!

Although I project the psalm onto a screen, I encourage participants to listen more than read. This is difficult for many people, but I remind them that hearing is how most Christians in history have engaged with the text of Scripture. I've also asked five of the small groups to read the psalm aloud in any fashion they wish, as long as everyone else can understand it.

## LECTIO DIVINA BEGINS

A volunteer opens with a prayer that the Holy Spirit will guide us through lectio divina, that we will be receptive to the Word, and that we will be changed by the word he has for each of us.

I tell people to sit in silence after the first two readings and pay attention to the one word or phrase that floats to the surface. "Look at the word or phrase in your mind from different angles. Shine a spotlight on every side of it. Chew on it with your mind. Flip it over and back again."

We sit in silence for a few moments before the psalm is read for the first time. A mother and daughter in the first small group read the psalm in unison. After a pause, an entire small group of middle school boys reads it together.

For me, the word is *enjoy*. Immediately my mind wants to rush ahead to talk to God about what this word means to me, and at points I catch myself thinking about the obvious implications for my faith: I need more joy. I should lighten up and enjoy God more. I have so much joy with my children, and that's a metaphor for how much God enjoys me. Each time I stop myself and move back to meditatio. This is seriously a spiritual discipline for me!

After about three or four minutes of silence, I say to them, "Go around and share your word or phrase with your group. No explanations, just the word or phrase that God has given you." I can hear people quietly saying phrases such as "far-flung peoples," "blessing," "enjoy you," "fair and square."

Then I say, "Now we will hear the psalm read two more times. This time, as you hear the psalm—especially the word or phrase you've just mentioned—pay attention to the feeling or emotion that it provokes in you. If God pulls you to another word or phrase, go with it. In the silence that follows, roll the word and the emotion around in your mind. Engage with the emotion, and let the word become a meditative mantra in your ear."

Another small group reads the psalm, this time two high school boys in unison. Then a man and woman in their twenties alternate stanzas, but they exclaim some words together (I've put these in roman):

> *God, mark us with grace*
> *and* blessing! Smile!
> *The whole country will see how you work,*
> *all the godless nations see how you save.*

*God! Let people thank and enjoy you.*
  *Let all people thank and enjoy you.*
*Let all far-flung people become happy*
  *and shout their happiness because*
*You judge them fair and square,*
  *you tend the far-flung peoples.*
*God! Let all people thank and enjoy you.*
  *Let all people thank and enjoy you.*
*Earth, display your exuberance!*
  *You mark us with blessing, O God, our God.*
*You mark us with blessing, O God.*
  *Earth's four corners — honor him!*


Even though it's not an emotion or feeling, with the word *enjoy* I experience a lightening — that is, I feel a lightness, like a lifting of weight off my shoulders. After three or four minutes of silence, I ask people to share, again without explanation, their words or phrases and the attached feelings with their small groups. In my small group, we share,

> *Far-flung people and lostness*
> *Enjoy and a lightening*
> *Enjoy you and happiness*
> *You judge and fear*

*Enjoy you and joy*
*Thank and enjoy you and gratitude*
*You save and hopefulness*

"Now," I tell the group, "we'll hear the psalm once more. After we hear it, we'll enter into a longer period of silence. During that time, try and move beyond words and images into a place of silence, even emptiness before God. Rest in God's love. Climb the ladder of divine ascent. Leave behind the things of this world, and with your mind and your heart, ascend into heaven. If you fall down a few rungs, or if words, images, or sounds flood your mind, don't get upset; just gently turn them away and begin again to ascend."

We sit in silence for maybe ten minutes. As the leader, I worry about the middle school boys and how they're dealing with this silence. Someone gets up and leaves the room. I worry that he's not having a good experience. (As it turned out, he went to the restroom.) Mainly I try to enter into contemplatio myself.

At the end of this silence, I ask everyone to slowly stand when they're ready, which allows people time to come out of contemplatio at their own pace. When everyone is standing, we recite the psalm once more and end the evening with the Lord's Prayer.

Some people trickle out as I turn the chant music back on, but most people sit back down in their small groups to debrief their experiences with lectio divina. It's important, especially for the first-timers, to have an opportunity to talk about the experience. "Was it difficult?" "Could you imagine trying it on your own at home?" "Should our small group try it again sometime?"

Finally, two and a half hours after beginning, I blow out the candles, turn out the lights, and just before locking the door, thank God for sending the Spirit to dwell among us on this night.

## A POSTSCRIPT

The next day I received word that Eric and Megan, volunteer leaders (among the best!) who had been at The Deepening the night before, had bad news. When Megan, five months pregnant, went for an ultrasound, they found out that their daughter Hannah, who suffered from a chromosome abnormality, had died in utero over the weekend.

Another pastor and I went to the hospital where Eric and Megan had checked in for Hannah's delivery. As we walked into their hospital room, Megan had her Bible open. "I'm just reading that psalm from last night," she said, "and remembering how good God is in the midst of all this pain." We prayed together, and we tried to thank God and enjoy him, even as we grieved the loss of Hannah.

# PART FOUR

# EXERCISES IN LECTIO DIVINA

On the following pages are a dozen passages from *The Message* for your own lectio divina, along with space for you to journal.

Having read this far, you should have a good grasp of the general lectio divina format. The four steps, as I have written about them, are only a guide. The point of lectio divina is to let God speak to you through his Word; however he guides you, go with it. The key is listening, so find a place and a time where you can be surrounded by quiet and immerse yourself in God's Word.

You might also want to look for a group in your area that practices lectio divina regularly—or start one yourself.

However you try it, may God bless you on this journey. I pray that you find lectio divina a helpful and wonderful way to enter more deeply than before into God's presence and gain an even bigger vision for his kingdom.

Peace.

**PSALM 23:1-3**

> GOD, *my shepherd!*
>> *I don't need a thing.*
> *You have bedded me down in lush meadows,*
>> *you find me quiet pools to drink from.*
> *True to your word,*
>> *you let me catch my breath*
>> *and send me in the right direction.*

Lectio — 10 minutes

Meditatio — 5 minutes

Oratio — 10 minutes

Contemplatio — 5 minutes

Journal about your thoughts and what God spoke to you through this word.

Close with the Lord's Prayer:

> *Our Father in heaven,*
> *Reveal who you are.*
> *Set the world right;*
> *Do what's best—*
> > *as above, so below.*
> *Keep us alive with three square meals.*
> *Keep us forgiven with you and forgiving others.*
> *Keep us safe from ourselves and the Devil.*
> *You're in charge!*
> *You can do anything you want!*
> *You're ablaze in beauty!*
> > *Yes. Yes. Yes.*

## MATTHEW 5:5

> *"You're blessed when you're content with just who you are—no more, no less. That's the moment you find yourselves proud owners of everything that can't be bought."*

Lectio—10 minutes

Meditatio—5 minutes

Oratio—10 minutes

Contemplatio—5 minutes

Journal about your thoughts and what God spoke to you through this word.

Close with the Lord's Prayer:

> *Our Father in heaven,*
> *Reveal who you are.*
> *Set the world right;*
> *Do what's best—*
> > *as above, so below.*
> *Keep us alive with three square meals.*
> *Keep us forgiven with you and forgiving others.*
> *Keep us safe from ourselves and the Devil.*
> *You're in charge!*
> *You can do anything you want!*
> *You're ablaze in beauty!*
> > *Yes. Yes. Yes.*

## 1 JOHN 3:1-3

*What marvelous love the Father has extended to us! Just look at it—we're called children of God! That's who we really are. But that's also why the world doesn't recognize us or take us seriously, because it has no idea who he is or what he's up to.*

*But friends, that's exactly who we are: children of God. And that's only the beginning. Who knows how we'll end up! What we know is that when Christ is openly revealed, we'll see him—and in seeing him become like him. All of us who look forward to his Coming stay ready, with the glistening purity of Jesus' life as a model for our own.*

Lectio — 10 minutes

Meditatio — 5 minutes

Oratio — 10 minutes

Contemplatio — 5 minutes

Journal about your thoughts and what God spoke to you through this word.

Close with the Lord's Prayer:

> *Our Father in heaven,*
> *Reveal who you are.*
> *Set the world right;*
> *Do what's best—*
> > *as above, so below.*
> *Keep us alive with three square meals.*
> *Keep us forgiven with you and forgiving others.*
> *Keep us safe from ourselves and the Devil.*
> *You're in charge!*
> *You can do anything you want!*
> *You're ablaze in beauty!*
> > *Yes. Yes. Yes.*

## JEREMIAH 2:2-3

> "Get out in the streets and call to Jerusalem,
>     'GOD's Message!
> I remember your youthful loyalty,
>     our love as newlyweds.
> You stayed with me through the wilderness years,
>     stuck with me through all the hard places.
> Israel was GOD's holy choice,
>     the pick of the crop.
> Anyone who laid a hand on her
>     would soon wish he hadn't.' "

Lectio — 10 minutes

Meditatio — 5 minutes

Oratio — 10 minutes

Contemplatio — 5 minutes

Journal about your thoughts and what God spoke to you through this word.

Close with the Lord's Prayer:

> *Our Father in heaven,*
> *Reveal who you are.*
> *Set the world right;*
> *Do what's best—*
>     *as above, so below.*
> *Keep us alive with three square meals.*
> *Keep us forgiven with you and forgiving others.*
> *Keep us safe from ourselves and the Devil.*
> *You're in charge!*
> *You can do anything you want!*
> *You're ablaze in beauty!*
>     *Yes. Yes. Yes.*

## LUKE 1:46-50

> *I'm bursting with God-news;*
>> *I'm dancing the song of my Savior God.*
> *God took one good look at me, and look what happened—*
>> *I'm the most fortunate woman on earth!*
> *What God has done for me will never be forgotten,*
>> *the God whose name is holy, set apart from all others.*
> *His mercy flows in wave after wave*
>> *on those who are in awe before him.*

Lectio—10 minutes

Meditatio—5 minutes

Oratio—10 minutes

Contemplatio—5 minutes

Journal about your thoughts and what God spoke to you through this word.

Close with the Lord's Prayer:

> *Our Father in heaven,*
> *Reveal who you are.*
> *Set the world right;*
> *Do what's best—*
> > *as above, so below.*
> *Keep us alive with three square meals.*
> *Keep us forgiven with you and forgiving others.*
> *Keep us safe from ourselves and the Devil.*
> *You're in charge!*
> *You can do anything you want!*
> *You're ablaze in beauty!*
> > *Yes. Yes. Yes.*

## COLOSSIANS 1:15

> *We look at this Son and see the God who cannot be seen. We look at this Son and see God's original purpose in everything created.*

Lectio — 10 minutes

Meditatio — 5 minutes

Oratio — 10 minutes

Contemplatio — 5 minutes

Journal about your thoughts and what God spoke to you through this word.

Close with the Lord's Prayer:

> *Our Father in heaven,*
> *Reveal who you are.*
> *Set the world right;*
> *Do what's best —*
>> *as above, so below.*
> *Keep us alive with three square meals.*
> *Keep us forgiven with you and forgiving others.*
> *Keep us safe from ourselves and the Devil.*
> *You're in charge!*
> *You can do anything you want!*
> *You're ablaze in beauty!*
>> *Yes. Yes. Yes.*

## DEUTERONOMY 32:1-4

> *Listen, Heavens, I have something to tell you.*
> > *Attention, Earth, I've got a mouth full of words.*
> *My teaching, let it fall like a gentle rain,*
> > *my words arrive like morning dew,*
> *Like a sprinkling rain on new grass,*
> > *like spring showers on the garden.*
> *For it is GOD's Name I'm preaching —*
> > *respond to the greatness of our God!*
> *The Rock: His works are perfect,*
> > *and the way he works is fair and just;*
> *A God you can depend upon, no exceptions,*
> > *a straight-arrow God.*

Lectio — 10 minutes

Meditatio — 5 minutes

Oratio — 10 minutes

Contemplatio — 5 minutes

Journal about your thoughts and what God spoke to you through this word.

Close with the Lord's Prayer:

*Our Father in heaven,*
*Reveal who you are.*
*Set the world right;*
*Do what's best—*
    *as above, so below.*
*Keep us alive with three square meals.*
*Keep us forgiven with you and forgiving others.*
*Keep us safe from ourselves and the Devil.*
*You're in charge!*
*You can do anything you want!*
*You're ablaze in beauty!*
    *Yes. Yes. Yes.*

## JOB 16:18-22

"O Earth, don't cover up the wrong done to me!
    Don't muffle my cry!
There must be Someone in heaven who knows the
truth about me,
    in highest heaven, some Attorney who can clear
my name—
My Champion, my Friend,
    while I'm weeping my eyes out before God.
I appeal to the One who represents mortals before
God
    as a neighbor stands up for a neighbor.


"Only a few years are left
before I set out on the road of no return."


Lectio—10 minutes

Meditatio—5 minutes

Oratio—10 minutes

Contemplatio—5 minutes

Journal about your thoughts and what God spoke to you through this word.

Close with the Lord's Prayer:

> *Our Father in heaven,*
> *Reveal who you are.*
> *Set the world right;*
> *Do what's best—*
> > *as above, so below.*
> *Keep us alive with three square meals.*
> *Keep us forgiven with you and forgiving others.*
> *Keep us safe from ourselves and the Devil.*
> *You're in charge!*
> *You can do anything you want!*
> *You're ablaze in beauty!*
> > *Yes. Yes. Yes.*

## ROMANS 15:13

*Oh! May the God of green hope fill you up with joy,*
*fill you up with peace, so that your believing lives,*
*filled with the life-giving energy of the Holy Spirit,*
*will brim over with hope!*

Lectio — 10 minutes

Meditatio — 5 minutes

Oratio — 10 minutes

Contemplatio — 5 minutes

Journal about your thoughts and what God spoke to you
through this word.

Close with the Lord's Prayer:

> *Our Father in heaven,*
> *Reveal who you are.*
> *Set the world right;*
> *Do what's best—*
> > *as above, so below.*
> *Keep us alive with three square meals.*
> *Keep us forgiven with you and forgiving others.*
> *Keep us safe from ourselves and the Devil.*
> *You're in charge!*
> *You can do anything you want!*
> *You're ablaze in beauty!*
> > *Yes. Yes. Yes.*

## ECCLESIASTES 11:9-10

*You who are young, make the most of your youth.*
*Relish your youthful vigor.*
*Follow the impulses of your heart.*
*If something looks good to you, pursue it.*
*But know also that not just anything goes;*
*You have to answer to God for every last bit of it.*


*Live footloose and fancy free —*
*You won't be young forever.*
*Youth lasts about as long as smoke.*


Lectio — 10 minutes

Meditatio — 5 minutes

Oratio — 10 minutes

Contemplatio — 5 minutes

Journal about your thoughts and what God spoke to you through this word.

Close with the Lord's Prayer:

> *Our Father in heaven,*
> *Reveal who you are.*
> *Set the world right;*
> *Do what's best—*
> > *as above, so below.*
> *Keep us alive with three square meals.*
> *Keep us forgiven with you and forgiving others.*
> *Keep us safe from ourselves and the Devil.*
> *You're in charge!*
> *You can do anything you want!*
> *You're ablaze in beauty!*
> > *Yes. Yes. Yes.*

## LEVITICUS 26:2-5

"Keep my Sabbaths; treat my Sanctuary with reverence. I am GOD.

"If you live by my decrees and obediently keep my commandments, I will send the rains in their seasons, the ground will yield its crops and the trees of the field their fruit. You will thresh until the grape harvest and the grape harvest will continue until planting time; you'll have more than enough to eat and will live safe and secure in your land."

Lectio — 10 minutes

Meditatio — 5 minutes

Oratio — 10 minutes

Contemplatio — 5 minutes

Journal about your thoughts and what God spoke to you through this word.

Close with the Lord's Prayer:

*Our Father in heaven,*
*Reveal who you are.*
*Set the world right;*
*Do what's best —*
*    as above, so below.*
*Keep us alive with three square meals.*
*Keep us forgiven with you and forgiving others.*
*Keep us safe from ourselves and the Devil.*
*You're in charge!*
*You can do anything you want!*
*You're ablaze in beauty!*
*    Yes. Yes. Yes.*

## REVELATION 22:20-21

> *He who testifies to all these things says it again:*
> "*I'm on my way! I'll be there soon!*"
> *Yes! Come, Master Jesus!*
> *The grace of the Master Jesus be with all of you.*
> *Oh, Yes!*

Lectio — 10 minutes

Meditatio — 5 minutes

Oratio — 10 minutes

Contemplatio — 5 minutes

Journal about your thoughts and what God spoke to you through this word.

Close with the Lord's Prayer:

> *Our Father in heaven,*
> *Reveal who you are.*
> *Set the world right;*
> *Do what's best—*
> > *as above, so below.*
> *Keep us alive with three square meals.*
> *Keep us forgiven with you and forgiving others.*
> *Keep us safe from ourselves and the Devil.*
> *You're in charge!*
> *You can do anything you want!*
> *You're ablaze in beauty!*
> > *Yes. Yes. Yes.*

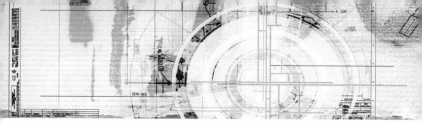

# NOTES

1. Thomas Aquinas, "Whether in Holy Scripture a word may have several senses?" in *Summa Theologica*, trans. by Fathers of the English Dominican Province (2nd and rev. ed., 1920; [online] ed. Kevin Knight, updated 2 December 2002 [cited 15 March 2003]); available from the World Wide Web at http://www.newadvent.org/summa/100110.htm

2. Helen Bacovin, trans., *The Way of a Pilgrim* and *the Pilgrim Continues His Way* (New York: Doubleday, 1978).

3. John T. McNeill, *The History and Character of Calvinism* (Oxford: Oxford Press, 1954), p. 336.

4. For example, Jesus quotes Psalm 22:1 in Mark 15:34 when he's dying on the cross. He uses Psalm 118:22-23 to refer to himself as the rejected capstone in Matthew 21:42, Mark 12:10-11, and Luke 20:17. In Matthew 13:35, he explains why he was teaching in parables by citing Psalm 78:2.

5. Benedicta Ward, *The Sayings of the Desert Fathers: The Alphabetical Collection* (Kalamazoo, Mich.: Cistercian, 1975), p. 3.

6. E. Kadloubovsky and G. E. H. Palmer, trans., *Writings from the Philokalia on Prayer of the Heart* (London: Faber and Faber, 1951), p. 92.

7. Anthony C. Meisel and M. L. del Mastro, trans., *The Rule of St. Benedict* (New York: Doubleday, 1975) pp. 86, 87.

8. Thomas Keating, "The Classical Monastic Practice of Lectio Divina," *Lectio Divina*, Winter 1998 [online, cited 15 March 2003]; available from the World Wide Web at http://www.centeringprayer.com/ lectio.htm

9. Michael Casey, *Sacred Reading: The Ancient Art of Lectio Divina* (Ligouri, Mo.: Ligouri/Triumph, 1995), p. 59.

10. *The Book of Common Prayer* (Oxford: Oxford University Press, 1979) contains the Lectionary for Sundays and the Daily Office. You can find *The Book of Common Prayer* online at http://justus.anglican.org/resources/bcp/lectionary.pdf. Print versions are available through your local bookstore. A Scripture lesson and related contemplative exercises are posted every day at http://www.sacredgateway.org

11. Eugene H. Peterson, "Words to Savor: Slow Down, You Read Too Fast," *The Christian Century* 119, no. 25 (4-17 December 2002), p. 18.

12. George Barna, "How America's Faith Has Changed Since 9-11," *Barna Updates*, 26 November 2001 [cited 15 March 2003]; available from the World Wide Web at http://www.barna.org/cgi-bin/PagePressRelease.asp?PressReleaseID=102&Reference=B

13. Quoted in Basil Pennington, *Lectio Divina: Renewing the Ancient Practice of Praying the Scriptures* (New York: Crossroad, 1998), pp. 160-161.

14. Thelma Hall, *Too Deep for Words: Rediscovering Lectio Divina* (New York: Paulist, 1988), p. 42.

15. William Johnston, ed., *The Cloud of Unknowing* (New York: Doubleday, 1973), ch. 3.

16. Johnston, ch. 17.

17. Johnston, ch. 71.

18. The word *catholic* refers to the universal church of the Lord Jesus Christ, not to the Roman Catholic Church.

19. Siur Marie Keyrouz, *Byzantine Chant—Passion and Resurrection*, Harmonia Mundi Franc—#901315, 1992.

20. Michael Casey, *Sacred Reading: The Ancient Art of Lectio Divina* (Ligouri, Missouri: Ligouri/Triumph, 1995), p. 59.

21. Kathleen Norris, *Amazing Grace: A Vocabulary of Faith* (New York: Riverhead, 1999), pp. 277-278.

# BIBLIOGRAPHY

Aquinas, Thomas. "Whether in Holy Scripture a word may have several senses?" in Translated by Fathers of the English Dominican Province, *Summa Theologica*, 2nd and rev. ed. (1920). Online edition edited by Kevin Knight, updated 2 December 2002 (cited 15 March 2003). Available from the World Wide Web at http://www.newadvent.org/summa/100110.htm

Bacovin, Helen, trans. *The Way of a Pilgrim and the Pilgrim Continues His Way*. New York: Doubleday, 1978.

Barna, George. "How America's Faith Has Changed Since 9-11." Barna Updates (26 November 2001) [cited 15 March 2003]. Available from the World Wide Web at *http://www.barna.org/cgi-bin/PagePressRelease.asp?PressReleaseID= 102&Reference=B*

*The Book of Common Prayer*, Revised 1979. Oxford: Oxford University Press, 1990.

Casey, Michael. *Sacred Reading: The Ancient Art of Lectio Divina*. Ligouri, Mo.: Ligouri/Triumph, 1995.

Hall, Thelma R. C. *Too Deep for Words: Rediscovering Lectio Divina with 500 Scripture Texts for Prayer*. New York: Paulist, 1988.

Johnston, William, ed. *The Cloud of Unknowing*. New York: Doubleday, 1973.

Kadloubovsky, E., and G. E. H. Palmer, trans. *Writings from the Philokalia on Prayer of the Heart*. London: Faber and Faber, 1951.

Keating, Thomas. "The Classical Monastic Practice of Lectio Divina." *Lectio Divina* (Winter 1998) [cited 15 March 2003]. Available on the World Wide Web at http://www.centeringprayer.com/lectio.htm

Keyrouz, Siur Marie. *Byzantine Chant—Passion and Resurrection*. Harmonia Mundi Franc—#901315. 1992.

Meisel, Anthony C. and M. L. del Mastro, trans. *The Rule of St. Benedict*. New York: Doubleday, 1975.

Norris, Kathleen. *Amazing Grace: A Vocabulary of Faith*. New York: Riverhead, 1999.

Pennington, M. Basil. *Lectio Divina: Renewing the Ancient Practice of Praying the Scriptures*. New York: Crossroad, 1998.

Peterson, Eugene H. "Words to Savor: Slow Down, You Read Too Fast." *The Christian Century* 119, no. 25 (4-17 December 2002), pp. 18-23.

Ward, Benedicta. *The Sayings of the Desert Fathers: The Alphabetical Collection*. Kalamazoo, Mich.: Cistercian, 1975.

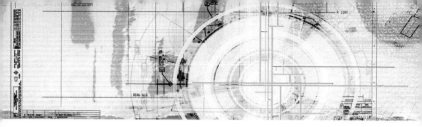

# AUTHOR

TONY JONES is the minister to youth and young adults at Colonial Church in Edina, Minnesota. In his years at Colonial, Tony has pioneered new forms of youth ministry, spending much of his time in one-on-one relationships with students. He has written numerous articles for publications such as *Youthworker Journal* and *Books & Culture*, and he is a featured writer on www.passageway.com, the teen Web site of the Billy Graham Evangelistic Association. He has authored several books, including *Postmodern Youth Ministry* (Youth Specialties/ Zondervan). Tony is married to Julie, and they have two children, Tanner and Lily. They live in Edina.

**Pray**
Tony Jones
1-57683-452-2

Do you ever feel a little stumped about prayer? Take a close look at some powerful prayers of the Bible and the early church, you'll see how effective prayer can be.

**Memorize This: TMS 3.0**
1-57683-457-3

How did Jesus handle temptation? He quoted God's Word in its face. A specialized version of NavPress' successful *Topical Memory System*, this book will help you deal with whatever life throws at you.

**The Message Remix**
Eugene H. Peterson
Hardcover
1-57683-434-4
Bonded Alligator Leather
1-57683-450-6

God's Word was meant to be read and understood. It was first written in the language of the people—of fishermen, shopkeepers, and carpenters. *The Message Remix* gets back to that feel. Plus the new verse-numbered paragraphs make it easier to study.

**Promises. Promises. Promises.**
Eugene H. Peterson
1-57683-466-2

Everybody's making promises these days.
But who's really true to their word?

God is. Take a look at His promises—promises of a real life and a future. See how knowing them can help you trust God even more.

**The Message:**
**The Gospel of John**
**in Contemporary Language**
Eugene H. Peterson
1-57683-432-8

Read what John witnessed as he walked alongside Jesus. Then help others find hope and a new way of life—better and more real than they've ever dreamed of experiencing. Share it with everyone you know!

*No games, no masks—God accepts us as we are.*

## Posers, Fakers, & Wannabes
Unmasking the Real You
Brennan Manning and Jim Hancock
1-57683-465-4

God isn't fooled by the games we play, the masks we wear. And as much as we try, we'll never fake our way into his affection.

The best part is: the Father already knows and accepts us exactly as we are. He knows how we think and act; He knows our dreams and fears. Brennan and Jim explain how God's total acceptance of us sets us free to be who we really are.

1-800-366-7788
www.th1nkbooks.com

THINK

**The Struggle**
Dr. Steven Gerali
1-57683-455-7
Available Fall 2003

Masturbation is a struggle for every guy. With this book, students will gain a biblical understanding on the topic and finally realize a freedom from their shame and guilt.

**The Chase**
Pursuing Holiness in Your Everyday Life
Jerry Bridges
1-57683-468-9
Available Fall 2003

Taken from the NavPress classic *The Pursuit of Holiness*, this book shows students how "running as to get the prize" isn't just possible, it's what life is all about.

1-800-366-7788
www.th1nkbooks.com

THINK